GOD
WHISPERS

BARBARA

MAY GODS
LIGHT BLESS
YOU & THOSE YOU LOVE

GOD
WHISPERS

Stories of the Soul, Lessons of the Heart

KARYN D. KEDAR

For People of All Faiths, All Backgrounds
JEWISH LIGHTS PUBLISHING
Woodstock, Vermont

God Whispers
Stories of the Soul, Lessons of the Heart

2000 First Quality Paperback Edition

In order to preserve my friends' and students' privacy, certain names have been changed.—KDK

Grateful acknowledgment is extended to the following for permission to reproduce their material in this book:

Random House, Inc./Alfred A. Knopf, Inc., for excerpt from *Wisdom of the Jewish Sages* by Rami M. Shapiro. Copyright © 1995 by Rami M. Shapiro. Reprinted by permission of Bell Tower, an imprint of Harmony Books, a division of Crown Publishers, Inc.

Jewish Lights Publishing, for excerpt from *Your Word Is Fire: The Hasidic Masters on Contemplative Prayer* © 1993 by Arthur Green and Barry W. Holtz (Woodstock, Vt.: Jewish Lights Publishing, 1993). Permission granted by Jewish Lights Publishing.

Liz Claiborne, Inc., for use of Vivid advertising copy.

Warner Books, for excerpt from *First You Have to Row a Little Boat* by Richard Bode. Copyright © 1993 by Richard Bode. By permission of Warner Books.

Library of Congress Cataloging-in-Publication Data
Kedar, Karyn D., 1957–
    God whispers : stories of the soul, lessons of the heart / Karyn D. Kedar
        p.   cm.
    ISBN 1-58023-023-7 (hc) 1-58023-088-1 (pb)
    1. Spiritual life—Judaism.   2. Self-actualization (Psychology)—
Religious aspects—Judaism.   I. Title.
    BM723.K35   1999
    296.7'2—dc21   98-43239
                                                                     CIP

10 9 8 7 6 5 4 3 2 1
Manufactured in the United States of America

Cover art and design by Drena Fagen
Text design by Susan Ramundo

For People of All Faiths, All Backgrounds
Published by Jewish Lights Publishing
A Division of LongHill Partners, Inc.
Sunset Farm Offices, Route 4, P.O. Box 237
Woodstock, Vermont 05091
Tel: (802) 457-4000 Fax: (802) 457-4004

www.jewishlights.com

To my parents, Lynore and Norman Schwartz,
whose gift of unconditional love taught me
the greatest truth of all.

CONTENTS

Elevated Thoughts

Balance

Sustainers

Surrender

Messages from God

Learning from Death

Choose Life

ACKNOWLEDGMENTS

Many of the ideas in this book were first conceived while I was teaching adult education for The Florence Melton Adult Mini-School in Florida and Chicago and in my classes at Congregation B'nai Torah. We engaged in serious learning, and my students pushed me to understand and explain complicated issues as I searched for answers and texts that inspire. There is great power in group study. The genius of the group is greater than that of any one individual. So if there is truth in these pages, it comes from the collective voice of all those who have engaged in conversation with me over the years. If it had not been for the questions, excitement, and love of learning by my students and those who let me into their lives at the most private of moments, I would still be silent and unable to find the words for the feelings that encompass my soul. I am truly grateful for my work at Congregation B'nai Torah. Through prayer, study, and conversation, I have connected with the stories and lives of people. Thank you for allowing me to become a small part of your search for meaning.

Many a lunch in Florida was spent with Rabbi Toba August discussing our understanding of the spirit and God. Rabbi August pushed and pulled at my thoughts and proved to me that although life can be tragic, one can triumph.

To all my teachers throughout the years, thank you. My teachers of literature, Dr. James Hill and Dr. Clarinda Lott, showed me the power and truth of metaphor, paradox, and irony. My teachers of the Bible, particularly Rabbi Chanan Brichto, may his memory be for a blessing, introduced me to a world of holy wonder. Baruch Krause uncovered the teacher within me and set me on a path of healing by insisting I know what I stand for. To Rabbi Barry Schwartz, Rabbi David Sofian, Gail Lipschitz, and Diane Velleto, you encouraged me to continue at critical junctures.

To Stuart Matlins, publisher of Jewish Lights, whose vision and courage is bringing a new voice to the world.

To my editor, Arthur Magida, thank you for knowing the difference between spirituality and cotton candy. Your talent and sensitivity make the process of editing an art.

I thank God for sending me teachers of the spirit in the form of Carol Dovi, Rabbi Charisse Kranes, may her memory be for a blessing, and most recently Lisa Fisher. These women are my sustainers. Carol was sent to me twenty-three years ago to set me on a spiritual quest. My life would be completely different without her. She is my friend, my teacher, my sister on a journey that is truly remarkable. From the pond to the heavens, thank you for being by my side. Charisse, may your song and genius continue to guide me as you parley with heavenly beings. And Lisa, thank you. Your help with the ideas of this book and the process of writing it was like pulling salt-water taffy: sweet, tough, fun.

To my family, I owe pages of gratitude. To my grandmother, Evangeline Dion Schwartz, your love of writing passed from the world of the spirit to the world in which I live. My parents made me believe that anything was possible even when life seemed impossible. My husband, Ezra, offered support and criticism in a way only a spouse dares. My children, Talia, Shiri, and Ilan, teach me love, adventure, and perspective.

To my adversaries, I offer my thanks. Through the struggle you have caused me, my path has emerged.

The most powerful prayer is a prayer of gratitude:
Blessed are You, God of my being,
Who has given me life,
Sustained me,
And brought me to this moment.

INTRODUCTION

I REMEMBER LYING ON MY front lawn as a child, feeling the grass as it pricked my back. I would listen to the sounds of my heart and the singing of birds, and I would wonder if all the meaning in the world could be found in the lacelike leaves that were set against the vast universe of sky as it changed colors from dawn to dusk.

As long as I can remember, I have searched to understand the ache in my soul, the elusive quality of joy, and the glue that connects us to one another. In my childhood search, I wrote stories and poems and drew diagrams of God and the spiritual world. As a child, I would observe my rabbi, Eugene Lipman of blessed memory, and I felt that he knew of things that were basic and essential. I wanted to know them, too. I would tag along to meetings at the synagogue with my father, enjoying the buzz of importance in the air. I loved to be near my Aunt Ivah Lee, who taught Sunday school and told me stories with authority and softness. I attended prayer services and watched my cousin Sharon sing with beauty and grace. I saw my mother and her family swear loyalty to family and the loving and complicated bonds it created. They told stories about their lives and encounters with others. I learned the difference between story and gossip, and I became a lover of the story that instructs great truths. I wanted to understand all these things with my mind and heart.

I suppose I have always been a seeker of wisdom, a struggler of the soul, and in search of beauty. This book is about what I have come to understand. It is about my journey to self-awareness and inner peace. It explores matters of the heart and soul and how they connect to all that is essential—to self, to family, to community, to God. As we increase the bonds of these connections through love, caring, faith, and giving, we increase our spiritual well-being. When we separate ourselves through guilt, fear, anger, or hate, we feel disconnected, alone, solitary, disfranchised. To embark on a spiritual journey, we must engage in two dances: one lessens fear, and one expands moments of love and connectedness. This book is about those dances, about the journey to spiritual awareness and understanding.

Here are the stories of ordinary people and their struggles with spiritual principles. These stories challenge us to befriend the strug-gle and see all the details of our lives as meaningful and sacred. They show us what is boldly personal and touch a universal cord that connects all people in our search for purpose and inner peace. As you read the pages of this book, notice your response to the spir-itual principles and the stories that illustrate them. If your eyes tear in recognition, listen to the truth that whispers to your soul. If your stomach tightens in fear, resist the urge to run, and return to that page another day. If you find words that anger you, step away for now, but know that you will be called again and again until you find the courage to hear about what angers you so.

God Whispers uses the ordinary to teach the extraordinary. We all teach what we need to learn. There is great integrity when we integrate our inner search to reflect our outward reach. There is an elegance and poetry when the seeker ventures to instruct others to better understand the very same lessons. The lessons in this book are for me as much as for others who might find them helpful. They give words to years of pondering and reflect the giddiness I feel when a new idea occurs to me. They are the result of years of teaching, reading, and searching. They are voices that would not be muted any longer.

THE DIVINE IN YOU

To be created in the image of God is
To come into this world with
A spiritual center
That is an avenue for Divine wisdom.
To find this center, listen to the silence.
Remember
To imagine, to dream, to envision
To create.

Recognize this internal beauty
As the holy within your being.
Act as if you are
Worthy of Divine command.

To be created in the image of God
Is to be granted a gift.

TELLING THE STORY OF YOUR LIFE

And you shall tell your children saying,
"This is what God has done for me."
—EXODUS 13:8

WHEN I WAS MAJORING in English literature as an undergraduate, studying literature was a mystical experience. Every story and every poem contained great eternal truths that filled my being with love and inspiration. I loved the study of literature. As the years progressed, I came to realize that what drew me to study literature was not necessarily the work itself but rather the literary conventions that commanded its form. I was in love with irony, metaphor, juxtaposition, and paradox. I quickly learned to apply these conventions to everything: to my life, to my study of scripture, to other people's lives. I saw everything as bits of one great story. My job as a seeker of Truth was to recognize the beauty of the metaphors and the mystery of the paradoxes. I began to listen intently to other people's stories, trying to render meaning from the details they chose to reveal. At first, I felt like a busybody. But then I realized that everyone has a story to tell. We shape our lives in the telling of our story. If we choose to recount the negatives in our life as a recurrent theme, then we have a certain perception of life. If we tell our story as if events and people are unconnected, we shape our ability to see meaning in events. If we tell our story as a series of blessings, then we have a certain outlook. There is great truth in the telling.

I was in search of wisdom.

I began to tell my story as if everything mattered, as if every detail had meaning, as if every event a purpose. I reconstructed the tale of my life as a master poet or novelist with plot and sequence, with meaning and metaphor. Irony has meaning; juxtaposition is revealing. Every character in fiction or in our life is there for a reason. I saw my life—and all life—as a great work in progress. My life is like an archetypal journey, and I am Huckleberry Finn, Moses, and Sarah. My journey has meaning; events happen for a reason; people come and go for a purpose.

As I retell my story in this way, the Why of my life takes form. It is given a voice. Connections are made between moments that were previously unrelated fragments. This way of seeing, this perspective, is vital to spiritual growth, since the details of our lives are not disparate moments or chance encounters.

Recently, I revisited a childhood memory that I rarely told anyone about because it was so painful. In the retelling, I discovered that the pain had given way to understanding. The twists and turns of our lives are meant to be. They teach us great truths if we can see them as part of a story that instructs. I decided to share the story with my students to illustrate how the events in our lives can be powerful metaphors for the essence of our being:

I was thirteen and it was the first winter I realized that the seasons were powerful metaphors for my inner life. It was lunchtime, and I clutched my crumpled brown lunch bag, stood at the door of the cafeteria, and looked for a place to sit. The tables were long pearl Formica tops with benches attached. At each table were clusters of kids eating, gossiping, giggling. My eyes scanned the cliques, only to see in their faces and bodies that I was not welcomed.

I had always been on the fringe. I was "different," living in an imaginary world that would someday be refined and admired as "creative." But in childhood it was painful to be "different." I remember in elementary school running to the playground during recess not wanting to play softball with the rest of the class. I would pretend that I was a wild mustang, running free and frantic, trying to escape roundup. I remember the teacher laughing and the children laughing. Perhaps it was the echo of their laughter from years past or perhaps I was still trying to escape "roundup," but that day at the door of the cafeteria, I felt that if I stayed and ate alone, all the cliques would taunt me for trying to make them feel sorry for me. So I turned around and let the heavy door slam behind me.

I walked toward the front doors of the school. It was winter and gray, and the ground was frozen mud. I opened the doors. A rush of ice-cold wind hit my face, and I saw sparrows trying to penetrate the hard earth for food. With these birds for my companions, I ate my lunch. I was terribly sad and lonely, but now I think that it was the beginning of my realization that there was depth to my soul and that if I wasn't afraid, it would lead me to God. It took over two decades to learn not to be afraid. In fact, what a wonderful metaphor for my life—a wild mustang learning to be free and unafraid.

When I finished telling the story, there was a silence. Embarrassed, I wondered if I had disclosed too much. The semester went on. At the last class, my students gave me a gift. I opened the small box and saw a beautiful sterling silver pin of wild horses running in the wind. I looked up at them with tears in my eyes. "We will never forget your story," they said. "It inspired us to become who we really are." When I need a reminder of the lesson, I wear the pin.

I search, as many of us do, for principles that connect, texts that inspire, metaphors that make us smile, analogies that make us sigh with understanding. And if I search with careful intent and yearning, I find the Divine within, nestled like pockets of love in these moments of connection, inspiration, and joy.

THE UGLY DUCKLING

And God said "Let there be light," and there was light . . .
In God's image they were created.
—GENESIS 1:3, 27

LIFE IS ENLIGHTENED BY particles of light rather than sunsets that take your breath away. You know the particles I mean. You're sitting at your kitchen table feeling rather mundane. Suddenly you look up, and a ray of sun catches the dust particles. They glimmer and twinkle and dance a scattered jig.

When we were living in Jerusalem, I would walk my daughter Shiri to school. The Jerusalem air was crisp and clear. The hustle and bustle of Israeli mornings did not affect us. We took our time, walking hand in hand. She looked up at me with a big smile and adoring eyes. I smiled at her.

She kept staring at me, and I said, "Why are you grinning at me like that?"

"Because your face is scrunched, and it's funny."

She was right. I was thinking of apartments yet to be bought and jobs yet to be had. A scrunched face is funny. I smiled at her wisdom.

She said, "Now you're beautiful."

"You're beautiful."

"You're amazing."

"You're incredible."

"Mommy?" Uh-oh, I thought, she's changing subjects.

"Where's the end of Israel?"

Shiri had been obsessed with the outer limits of comprehension, with the last number, with what is beyond the world, and now with the borders of Israel.

So I told her, and she said, "Can we go to the sea? I want to see the end of Israel."

"Sure," I said, glad she didn't ask to go to Syria.

"Mommy, how do you know everything?"

"I listened to my teachers, and I read a lot of books."

"Mommy, what am I going to be when I grow up? Anything I want?"

"Yes, Shiri, anything you want."

"I want to be a rabbi like you, but where do you get the clothes?"

"You mean the robes? They give them to you at work."

"Actually," she said, "I don't know what I want to be."

There was a small silence, and I looked at her face. It was scrunched.

"Maybe I'll be nothing," she said.

"You'll always be something," I replied. "You'll always be Shiri Lee. And that is very special."

Her smile returned, and we entered the school.

"Mommy, give me a bear hug and a bunny kiss. I'll show you how."

Yes, I thought as I walked home, I'll always be me, and that is something special. It was the first time I had thought of myself in that way. I had measured my worth through my work, through the grand colorful sunsets of crowds cheering me on. But now I think that life is sweetest when you see particles of light dancing amid the mundane.

How do I discover my good? How do I define my worth? Somewhere deep in my soul, God keeps telling me that I am in an image that is Divine and that is the highest level of being that is possible. Somewhere in my mind, I fight this fact. All I know is that I must take more lessons from my children, lessons about bear hugs and bunny kisses, about self-love that is unconditional.

This is our mission: recognizing the Divine within. We must define ourselves by that Divine image, by that light that burns deep inside. What others say of us is important. It reflects our good name, our reputation. What others think can advance us or keep us out of where we want to go.

But what others think does not give us peace of spirit. It does not quiet our souls and mind. It does not make us spiritually healthy. What we think of ourselves can do all that. It is so simple, yet at times so elusive.

I have always loved the story "The Ugly Duckling," and I vividly remember the movie "Hans Christian Anderson," with Danny Kaye. Remember how he brings the bald child close to him and begins to sing the ugly duckling song? I will never forget that child. I found it curious that he was bald, but I never saw him as ugly. When the children from the town gathered round to hear the story, it became clear that the story was for each of them. And as Danny Kaye sang, I knew the story was for me, too.

In the early years of my rabbinate, I was often asked to speak about women in the rabbinate. I always resented these talks. I felt that women's ordination was too new for me to analyze it as phenomenon. I felt uncomfortable talking about myself in the third person (she) and about other women rabbis whom I didn't know in the second person (you). So I began simply to tell my story. I always began with a detailed retelling of "The Ugly Duckling." I would get to the end of the story, pause for dramatic effect, and then announce that life as a female rabbi was like life as the ugly duckling. Does she quack? Does she dive for fish? She doesn't look like a rabbi, I mean, a duck.

The truth is that all of us live a life that invites us to journey toward beauty. As we struggle through our early years, we play a game of conform/rebel. The balance between these two forces depends on the spiritual deepening we do. If we mostly conform, we lose the uniqueness of who we are. If we mostly rebel, we act in anger over the fact that we are forced to conform. But as we journey toward self-awareness, we discover that our uniqueness is a gift from God. We need not conform or rebel, which is how we react to what others say and demand. Rather, as the poet e.e. cummings writes, "it takes courage to grow up and turn out to be who you really are." We are not ugly at all, but rather that most beautiful of creatures. Our task is to find the path to that beauty.

Each of us is unique. This is not merely a line we tell our children. It is true. Find your Truth and live there. When you do, you will bathe in the particles of God's light.

THE SONG OF THE ASCENT

We are as dreamers
Our mouths are filled with laughter
Our tongues, with songs of joy.
—PSALM 126:1, 2

THERE IS A SONG as you ascend toward that secret vision of who you are. It sings with the sweetness of heaven. I hear it play from within with the power of a symphony and the simplicity of a single melody. I hear the song when I dream of who I could be. I hear the song when I imagine how my life will be. I become the song when I create all that I have dreamed, imagined, and envisioned. When I become my dreams, I live to the rhythm of the Divine reason for my life. When I don't, my soul is painfully silent.

I have witnessed this silence. It is the void in our lives that we believe would be filled if we only knew what to do with our days. It may be a dissatisfaction with work or with our daily routines. The mistake we make is that we believe that the cure is in the *doing* of something right, while it is really in the *being* of who we are. Somewhere along the way, someone told us that we shouldn't or couldn't or really can't be who our soul longs to be. So we became who we thought we should be—accountants, homemakers, doctors, or whatever—and lost our authentic selves. We feel trapped in our lives. The soul does not sing. We lose a sense of who we are and why we are.

There was a story told by Rebbe Nachman of Breslov from the eighteenth century:

> Long ago, in a faraway land, there was a strange type of mold that affected the grain in the fields. The king knew that if his people ate this grain, they would lose their mind and go mad. He discussed the problem with his chief advisor, and they decided to use the grain in the storehouses while trying to find a remedy for the afflicted grain. Time passed and the store-houses were empty, but still no remedy was found. The king decided that it was better to feed his people grain that would make them lose their mind than to let them die of starvation.
>
> "I too will eat of this grain," he told his advisor, "so that I will be like my people—lost in madness. From that shared place, I will be able to lead them."
>
> "But what of me?" said the advisor. "I will advise you, but you will not understand me."
>
> "You too must eat of the grain," said the king, "but there is one more thing. Before we eat this grain, I will order all my people to put a mark on their forehead. Every morning, they must look at their reflection and see this mark and ask them-selves who they really are."

This is how the story ends, and this is how it ends for many of us. Having been fed the stuff that shatters dreams, we are left wonder-ing who we would be if we were in our right mind. What would life be like if we followed our dreams and visions of who we yearn to be? Through these dreams and visions we find our mark; the Divine purpose of our lives is revealed to us.

Make your dreams a thing of beauty. They are what is possible when barriers are removed and obstacles disappear. To dream is not to fantasize. To dream is to create first in the heart, then in the mind, and then in the world in which we live.

HOPE

The psalmist cries,
"O God of all being, my God
I have cried out to You
And You have healed me.
Weeping may linger in the night
But at dawn there is joy."
—Psalms 30:3, 6

Hope is the bridge
To the next stage of your life.
Go forward
With hope in your heart,
You will not fall.

CREATING SANCTUARY

Make for Me a Sanctuary and I shall dwell among you . . .
Make two cherubim of gold at the two ends of the entrance . . .
The cherubim shall have their wings spread out above.
They shall be turned toward one another,
Their faces turned toward the entrance.
—EXODUS 25:8, 18, 20

WE MUST CREATE POCKETS of hope, safe places where pain is softened because love abounds, places where God is invited to fill the void, where sparks of kind light banish the darkness. Once we find these places, we must surrender to their safety.

The desert: vast, loudly quiet, beautiful, dangerous. The desert journey: mysterious, endless directions, no clear path. The vast horizons of the desert make me dizzy and confuse me as to which way I should go. God says, "Build Me a Sanctuary so that I might dwell among you," and I get busy building a structure that will symbolize God's presence and love. I am commanded to focus on the details: blue, purple, and crimson yarns; acacia wood; pure gold, dolphin skins, and lapis lazuli. My focus gives me direction. It gives me hope that I will be guided out of the desert. I build this sanctuary, and I feel safe. As I approach the sanctuary, I feel God's presence, and I see the great cherubim guarding the entrance. I see their faces turned ever so slightly so that their gazes meet as I enter. "Where is God?" I ask myself. Perhaps God is in the place that their gazes meet.

I was searching for God in the numb stare of the thirteen-year-old girl in my office. She was about to become bat mitzvah, that rite of passage in which a young teen leads the congregation in worship and enters the community as a responsible adult. But before me was a sad, unresponsive, and aloof child. I had been hearing rumblings about her family. A recent divorce had left the husband stunned. Both parents agreed, however, to present a unified front when it came to the children, so both sat in my office with their daughter. I looked at Ivy's mother. She was beautiful, vivacious, filled with joy and life. I looked at her father. He was quiet, unsure, and terribly sad. I searched Ivy's face and saw both those forces living in her. She had not yet decided which would dominate her life. It was clear that she was not able to deal with the pressures of the approaching service and found the whole event terribly irrelevant to her difficult life.

I tried to engage Ivy in conversation, but mostly she stared blankly and gave me one-word answers. Occasionally, she would look at her parents and check their reactions against what I had said. I finally asked her parents to leave the room.

The door closed. I smiled at Ivy to assure her she was not "in trouble."

"Parents divorced this year?" I said in a matter-of-fact voice.

"Yeah." I could barely hear her.

"It's been tough, huh?"

"Uh-huh."

"This service doesn't mean much to you right now, huh?"

"I guess not."

I decided to continue with blunt honesty. "I suppose I understand that. It must be weird to be the center of all this attention when you feel your world is falling apart."

She looked at me carefully, trying to decide if she could trust me. She slid further into her seat and said, "Yeah, it's really weird."

"It's OK, Ivy. We'll get through this together. I'll be right by your side. You will get through this. You can't fail. I won't let you."

She slowly smiled at me, and I saw her beauty and sweetness. The day of the service arrived, and the guests were dressed in shades of elegance. Ivy was sitting by herself in my office, hiding from the turmoil outside. I sat with her and went over the last-minute details. She left the office to greet her guests, and I stood at the door and watched. Moments before we were to begin, people were entering the sanctuary, and Ivy's father came up to her to wish her well. As he leaned down to kiss her, she rested her head against his chest and burst into tears. Her mother saw what was happening from afar but was too stunned to react. As her father put his arms around her, she pulled away. I then took her by the arm into my office and closed the door.

I took both of her hands in mine. They were cold and fragile. I looked into her eyes and said, "Ivy, I want you to remember this moment. At this moment, you are loved and honored for who you are. You are not alone. I am here for you, and God is always with you. If you are ever in trouble, even ten years from now, you come to me. You are safe, Ivy. It will be OK. Let's begin the service."

Trembling, she did not want to pull her hands away. We had built a sanctuary of safety and invited God to dwell among us. We stared into each other's eyes, and in the place our gazes met, God brought us warmth, safety, and love. She surrendered to a moment of hope, and we left to lead the service.

In our sadness and fear of the future, we must find hope. We must be able to envision ourselves in a safer place, where we are loved for who we are and who we are meant to be.

THE WEDDING

Do not despair because of suffering,
For life is suffering.
Suffering and also joy.
When life brings you suffering, hurt.
When life brings you joy, laugh.
Cling to nothing
For all is fleeting.
—MISHNAH AVOT 1:7

SHE VOWS TO LIGHT a candle. Sitting by the grave of her mother as the body is lowered into the ground, she says a prayer so silent that her heart barely hears its cry. Her mother died of cancer, and she, too, is now struggling with the disease. She hasn't told anyone yet that she is sick with the disease that killed her mother, but she makes a vow to fight harder than anyone can imagine. She vows to fight in memory of her mother, who lost her battle. She vows to fight in hope that her daughter will not be sitting by the grave of *her* mother, as she is now. Her prayer is for the strength and courage it takes to win.

Five years later, her wedding day approaches. It is a second marriage for both of them. They have struggled with health, trust, intimacy, and hope. Hope that love abides, hope that they chose wisely this time. I have watched them for a year now. Together, they have children whose ages span two decades and some very heavy baggage. They are very serious in their reaching for love. They are determined to make it work. They have talked, cried, fought, and loved hard. Now, they are ready to recite wedding vows. There is great joy in their faces; there is deep humility in their love.

Her wedding day has arrived. I meet her in the parking lot as she slides out of the minivan in her long white gown. She mentions her mother and begins to cry uncontrollably. I take her hand and lead her to the sanctuary. During the quiet moments before the ceremony, with her family and her fiancé present, we say a prayer:

> God, help us to understand
> That everything in our lives,
> The good, bad, and the ugly
> Have led us to this moment right now.
> Be with us as we embrace it all,
> The tears and the joy.
> All that has come before
> Is the path that has blessed us with this moment.

She walks quickly down the aisle with her children pulling at her side. We begin the ceremony by lighting two candles. The first we light in memory of her mother. The second we light for the beauty and love of the moment and to provide light for her children in the future. They exchange vows, kiss, and the entire congregation explodes with applause and tears.

They have taught us that hope is the very foundation of a life worth living.

I gaze upon them and I see the light of God's presence.

STEPPING INTO YOUR LIFE

And there he came to a cave
And he slept there. And God came to him and said,
"What are you doing here, Elijah?"
"I have been zealous for God . . ." And God said,
"Go forth and stand upon the mountain before God."
—1 Kings 19:9, 11

WHEN I STAND BEFORE God, where do I stand? I may be looking at a magnificent sunset or be in a place of worship. I may be gazing into my child's eyes as she comes into my bed for an early-morning snuggle. I am before God when I am at the brink of stepping into my life determined to leave a period of numb existence.

When I stand before God, I stand in the light of hope.

I may hear a voice from within urging me to go from the dark cave into the light. The cave is safe, familiar, known. To venture to the edge of what I have become accustomed to feels dangerous. It would mean stepping into the unknown. Sometimes our fears paralyze us. We don't make changes in our lives because we fantasize about the ramifications of our true desires. A myriad of "what ifs" keeps us from moving forward. "I can't change careers at my age," a man recently said to me. "I am more than miserable. I go to work every day and feel like I am going to die." But instead of supporting our fears, what if we support our dreams? "Why can't you change careers?" I ask. "You are bright enough to figure that out."

When I stand before God, I stand at the edge of my limitations.

I look out as far as I can see, and I know that anything is possible. Anything. To be free, I need only take a step—any step. I am scared, since it feels like I might fall. But rather than cling to these fears, I prefer clinging to the image of a hang glider. Running on a large flat plateau with bright yellow wings fastened on her back, the pilot of the glider runs as fast as she can. She does not hesitate or look back or slow down. She reaches the edge of the plateau and flies. So all I need are wings of faith and the desire to race to the edge of the mountain, then . . . Oh my God, I can fly.

I can not fail when I stand before God
For if I fall I will land
In the hands of God.
For if I fall I know I can
Find enough strength, enough love
And happiness to keep me up,
For You, dear God, are by my side.
For if I fall I will still live.
—Talia Kedar, age 13

PATIENCE

Steady yourself. Living takes time.
Each moment is a moment to be lived.
Each emotion is to be felt.
We are here in this world to learn and grow.
Fear can teach. Confusion instructs. Sadness informs.
Love elevates.
Take the time to experience each breath,
Especially the ones that make you want to run.

Patience. Steady.
Rush and race banish joy and peace.
There is wonder to experience if you take the time.
Step softly and deliberately.
What lingers must be lived and
Once lived completely passes in its own time.
To force the natural rhythms of life
Is to deny yourself of the
Divine wisdom in each experience.

HIDE-AND-SEEK

They heard the voice of God walking in the Garden
toward the cool of day.
And the Man and the Woman hid themselves from the presence of God
Among the trees of the Garden.
God called out to Man and said, "Where are you?"
And he said, "I heard your voice in the Garden
and I was afraid because I was naked
And I hid myself."
—GENESIS 3:8–10

HAVE YOU EVER PLAYED hide-and-seek with God? You hide that moment that you realize that you are naked and you are afraid to love the essence of yourself in the light. You hide from yourself; and you hide from God because you are afraid that the truth about who you are will be too horrible to bear. You do not want to be discovered. What if you are an impostor? You are not who everyone thinks you are. Worse, you are not really who you pretend to be. What if you look different in the light of the Garden?

I stare at the freshly painted walls in my small apartment and become angry with my daughter for the black smudge of dirty fingers. She doesn't understand my wrath. It is in her nature to touch and grab and stroke the dirt of the universe. Dirty fingerprints are the signatures of a hungry soul. She is so smart and sure, so she grabs at it all because she knows that life belongs to those who grasp. Children are true to themselves, even when it annoys Mommy and Daddy. Children know who they are. They live their authentic selves. They know how to live boldly. A child doesn't really care that adults say "no." They care mostly about themselves. They simply live by a higher command—be who you are; laugh when happy; cry when sad; scream when angry. We tell them this is wrong, because this is what we were told. And so we grow up and we learn to behave and to please others.

All this is very civilized, but it can cause the submergence of the true self. When we are mostly motivated by the frown of the parental finger waving in our face, we lose the energy that comes from courage, innocence, and self-love. Fear of disapproval makes us go into hiding. Forgetting to please ourselves makes us hide. I remember when I began to hide. I was a teenager, upset that my friends seemed to be distancing themselves from me. I wanted their friendship, yet I didn't want to compromise myself. I was outside; the autumn air was a bit too cool. I'd forgotten my sweater. The sun was tucked behind the trees. I remember a strange feeling. It was as if the footsteps of God's voice were following me from behind. That is when I began to hide. I hid because I was scared to be caught naked and vulnerable. I was afraid that the sight of my true self would be grotesque. I ran and hid among giant imaginary evergreens.

It is the hide-and-seek of a vulnerable soul. I had begun to create myself, not in the image of God, but in the image of delusion. Creating a person who I thought would be better liked and respected, I pretended to be a bit smarter and a lot tougher. I did not show others my weaknesses. I carefully chose who I loved and who I allowed to love me. It was a game that lasted for years. I thought it was better this way. Life turned so cold that it was as if I had tied a gray scarf around my neck to keep me warm. All it did was choke the giddiness out of an honest life. There were always fears of being discovered as an impostor. I would say to myself, "If you really knew me . . ."

It seems that hide-and-seek is a natural first response to our insecurities. Years of hearing "No, you can't," "Stop, don't do that," and "Try harder" make us afraid to venture. But the game is not just "hide"; it is also "seek." Discern when to listen, when to defy, when to modify, and never act from fear. Come out into the light. When you hear the voice of God, don't be afraid. Answer as the ancient Hebrews did when God called to them: *heneni,* "I am here." Do not hide. You are beautiful and perfect even when you are naked and especially when you are vulnerable. You are in God's image. Come into the light and see the innocence of your younger years. Dig deep, for the earth of your soul is rich and fertile, and the dirt under your nails is from Holy ground. Try playing tag instead of hide-and-seek. You're "it." Have patience. As time passes, you will be found.

CONFUSION

Blessed are You who open the eyes of the blind.
—MORNING PRAYERS

As soon as I reached the open water,
I found myself faced with a familiar dilemma;
This freedom I cherished came with a precondition,
I had to decide where I wanted to go.
—RICHARD BODE, *FIRST YOU HAVE TO ROW A LITTLE BOAT*

THE STORY IS TOLD of the ancient Israelites wandering in the vastness of the desert not knowing which way to go. God told them that they would be guided by the Divine Presence. They should follow a pillar of cloud by day and a pillar of fire by night. When the cloud descended upon the people, it would be a sign to camp, not to journey on until it lifted.

As I explore the vast possibilities that life brings, I am at times confused, as if I am in a cloud and unable to see the way. During those moments, I know I should pause and reflect and have patience. It is uncomfortable being in a cloud, in a haze of thought. But these moments are when I can shift into new directions, bring new dimensions into my life. If I run, I will be lost. If I wait and let the confusion and anxiety settle, then the cloud lifts, pointing toward a way that is clear.

It is possible that confusion just may be an unrecognized moment of clarity. Suddenly, my eyes open and I see that all is possible and that life is filled with endless variety. In this moment of clarity, I know that the future holds a thousand renditions of what might be and a million possibilities of what may never be. As my mind races through these, my eyes cloud, my stomach tightens, my head enters a dense fog. I squint and try to focus on all the "maybes" and "why nots" and "what ifs." Anything is possible, and I am confused as to what is fundamental, essential, right.

A student in my adult education class asked me to lunch recently. We chatted about our children, our husbands, our work. There was a pause. I took a long sip of my raspberry iced tea, thinking how clever it was to combine fruit flavor and tea and ice. I looked up at my companion. Her face seemed relaxed in deep thought. "You know," she said softly, "of all the lessons you taught last year, the one about the cloud has really helped me. When I do not know what to do or where to go, I see the cloud of God surround me, and I simply wait." It was her turn to sip tea, as I quietly thanked God for moments of calm and faith.

When the cloud descends, still your instinct to run or flee. Stay quiet and make no decisions while you are in the cloud. Be patient and know that as you squint and toss and turn, God is with you in the cloud. And when it lifts, you may journey on.

BUILD YOURSELF AN ARK

God said to Noah, "Build yourself an Ark.
Make an opening for daylight to come through."
—GENESIS 6:13–14, 16

THERE ARE TIMES THAT I am truly lost and overwhelmed and seem to be incapable of knowing the way to joy. It is as if a strong wave has sent me tumbling to the ocean floor. "Don't panic," I remember my swimming teacher saying. "If you don't panic, you will float to the top." How can I be patient when I feel as though I am drowning?

It was early in the morning. I had been asked to lead an informal study session about the story of Noah at the national convention of The Association of Reform Zionists of America. I surveyed the group, wondering who had come and what they had come to hear. As I reached for the thick Bible commentary that I would be using for the discussion, I asked that we open to the appropriate page. The book was clumsy and heavy. I turned to the portion, looked at the words, and began to teach. As I was teaching, a soft, loving voice came through me. I said: There are truly times when you are suffocating, as if in a flood of inescapable sadness. There are times when you feel as if you are under a deep dark ocean. You must learn to build an ark to protect yourself from drowning. Just as in the story, this ark is made with the specifications of wisdom, to be an ark that will float and not leak. And God said, "Make a window so the daylight can come through." Always have an opening, a window, however small, where the light can shine through. And know, from within your ark, that there will be a moment when you must emerge. You may need help knowing when to come out. Have patience. Send a white dove to find green peacefulness. Have a friend who will search for dry ground for you. She may come back with nothing at first. Life is a process. It takes time. But she will come back and beckon you through that small window toward the door. It's OK to be shaken. You have been floating awhile, but know that every rainbow shines with the many colors of survival.

Then I sat down, breathing ever so slowly. I continued the lesson.

ACTS OF LOVING-KINDNESS

The world stands
Upon acts of loving-kindness
—Mishnah Avot 1:2

Careful,
Not everything you do
Is in the name of self.
The Hebrew word matzpoon *means*
Conscience, north, and compass all in one.
Listen to your conscience.
It is your compass,
Your North Star.
It will guide you when the night is dark.
It will point you to safety.
It will keep you true to yourself.
It will ask you to extend a hand.

Never betray your sense of right.

The self can not truly be full
Without tending to the needs of others.
We live in relationship, not in isolation.
Our quest for kindness and love
Must extend beyond the walls of self
To the hearts and minds of others.

Give and you get in the most fundamental way.

ACTS OF DIVINE KINDNESS

With love and grace You sustain the living
You support the falling,
Heal the sick,
Free those who are bound in captivity,
And keep faith with those who sleep in the dust.
—THE AMIDAH, A DAILY PRAYER

WE ARE CREATED IN the image of God, so I must behave in the same ways in which I describe God's power. As God sustains the world, so must I, with actions that nourish the soul. Just as I ask God to support those who fall from hope into despair, so do I reach out to those who are too weak to stand without the support of another. I must tend to those whose body and spirit are sick. Their cry of pain must be my summons to help. As I witness the knot in the soul of my friend that is tied so tightly that she is her own prisoner, I must help her to unravel it and free the strands of beauty and brilliance that are truly her core. And as for the soul that sleeps, I urge and prod her gently, encouraging her to live fully and gloriously.

As I understand the nature of God, so must I understand my role in the world.

I was invited to speak about spirituality to a small group of women. There were fewer than ten of us sitting around a dining room table. For the first twenty minutes or so they listened politely. Then one of the women, who was in her late sixties, couldn't stand it anymore. She sat up straight in her chair and blurted out, "I don't get this spiritual stuff. In my day, we did not have time to feel lost or dwell on our problems. There were things to be done. When we wanted to get involved, we joined the temple's social action committee. We marched for civil rights. We fought to free the Jews from the former Soviet Union. We fed the hungry. Don't you think you young people are a little self-obsessed? If you are depressed or sad, do something for someone else."

She was right. Acts of loving-kindness transform our soul and fix a bit of a broken world. A sense of spiritual well-being comes from connecting to others, to God, to love. The belief that behavior modification changes a person is not only from the world of psychology. The religious belief in "commandment" stems from the understanding that as I do, I also become. If I give, I will become giving. If I love, I will become loving. If I help to heal others, I will heal myself. The spiritual path must extend beyond the private world of self into the chaotic world of others. If you extend acts of kindness, you bring a loving order to the chaos.

There was a moment in my life that was so defining that I was forever transformed. Oddly enough, I do not remember the circumstances or even where I was. What I do remember was a pain that was so deep that it exhausted my very soul. "Kindness," I said. "I just want more kindness in my life." From the first moment that I uttered those words, I must have said them and acted them out a thousand times until finally they became true and there *was* more kindness in my life. I am now a kinder person. And I am surrounded by love and kindness. I strive to perform acts of love as a daily spiritual practice and out of a sense of Godly command. As I do, I draw to myself loving, kind people.

May these kindnesses continue to increase and transform my world and the corner of it that I touch.

REPAIRING
A BROKEN WORLD

It is incumbent upon us
To praise God
Who has formed all of creation.
To repair the world . . .
To bring us nearer to the day
That the world will be one.
—THE ALEINU PRAYER

JEWISH MYSTICS SAY THE world is broken, shattered from the very beginning of creation itself. God's light is scattered, and pieces of it can be found everywhere. Our task is to put it back together again, shard by shard, spark by spark. This is called *tikkun olam*—"fixing the world"—and we can do it by following commandments: those Godly imperatives like giving, compassion, justice, acts of loving-kindness. They are the law of life. The more Godly imperatives we take upon ourselves, the more repair we accomplish. By fixing a corner of the world, we mend an aspect of ourselves.

7:00 P.M.: The witching hour in a home with children. In a short period of time, homework must be completed, baths taken, stories told, and dishes cleaned; the inevitable crisis must be solved; lights must go out, and little lives must surrender to sleep.

Precisely in the middle of all this chaos, I receive a phone call: "Rabbi, I need your help. I am a victim of the flood that happened a few weeks ago in the neighboring town. I came to your area thinking I was going to meet someone who would give me a place to stay, and he didn't show up. I'm out of money and need some cash so I can spend the night in a hotel." Shiri was asking me a question about her math homework. I referred the caller to Jewish Family Services, which is equipped to help such cases. He called back: they had gone home for the day. From upstairs, my son Ilan called from the tub: the water was too cold. I told the caller about a police emergency fund. He called back: they did not have such a fund. Ilan was now running around naked looking for clean underwear, and Talia wanted to discuss an article she had read in *Seventeen* magazine about date rape. The man on the phone sounded as if he really needed help, but I couldn't be sure. I remembered that a close friend's ex-husband had become mentally ill and was living on the streets. She had said, "I hope someone extends him a periodic kindness to ease his way."

I finally gave in. I said to my husband that chances are he will use the money for liquor, but then there was the slight possibility that he was legitimately in need. I sent my husband to the parking lot where the man was calling from with enough money for a night in a hotel. He came home and said, "There was alcohol on his breath." We had played the odds and lost.

Or is it ever possible to lose when we give? I had given because the very act of giving transforms me and a bit of the world. If giving is not my first impulse, then I become more self-absorbed—and the world loses as one more soul retreats from it. Divine sparks remain scattered.

After telling this story in a sermon, a congregant told me, "I am an oral surgeon, and I get four or five calls a night. I understand that people are in real pain and that they need me. I am good until the fifth call. I just have no more to give. Now I realize that's the call that God has sent me."

I looked at him and understood the true meaning of that night when the man called asking for money for a hotel room. I had been so tired and so depleted that my thoughts had become my prayer and God had heard them. "You think you can't give anymore," God was telling me. "Here, give anyway."

The cure for spiritual depletion is not hibernation. The cure is to be engaged with the world. Reach out to the stranger. Extend your hand to someone whose inner resources are even more depleted than yours. Giving creates wholeness in yourself and the world you touch. Opening your arms to embrace another person leaves you open for a loving embrace in return. If you feel lost, find a friend in need. If you feel poor, give to someone else. If you feel anguish, soothe another's pain.

If the world is broken, the mystics say, fix it. In this way you mend your spirit and eventually the world.

THE PENNY

Judah ben Tema said:
Be strong as a leopard,
Light as an eagle,
Swift as a deer,
And brave as a lion
When carrying out tasks of righteousness.
—WISDOM OF THE JEWISH SAGES 5:23,
TRANSLATED BY RABBI RAMI SHAPIRO

I BELIEVE THAT A SENSE of abundance is mostly based on belief and not reality. I know couples who have totally different perceptions of their assets. The husband believes that there is never enough, and the wife believes that there is more than plenty. I know parents who teach their children that they must always save money and things—even people's love—because we're always in danger of running short. I have heard stories from adult children who grew up poor, yet they'd always had a feeling of plenty: plenty of food, plenty of room for guests, plenty of love to go around. Abundance is a matter of worldview.

I was preparing my sermons for the High Holy Days. Hundreds of people come to these services, and there is great pressure to deliver a meaningful message. The week before the holiday, I heard a Hasidic tale about a young man who had been kidnapped by an evil tax collector. The young man's wedding day was quickly approaching, and the community did not know what to do. They decided to pay the ransom, but the only one who could afford it was the miser who lived on the edge of town. Despite the warnings that the rich man never gave away any of his fortune, the rabbi went with his students to his home to ask for money. He knocked on the miser's door and told him about the lad who had been kidnapped shortly before his wedding day. The miser was moved to tears and ran to get some money. When he returned, the rabbi saw that the miser's clenched fist was shaking. The miser slowly opened his fist. In it was one small, dirty old penny. The rabbi took the penny and began to thank the man and bless him profusely: "May God grant you health and long life. May you live a life of joy worthy of heaven. May God increase the love in your life."

The students of the rabbi looked at him as if he was crazy. After all, the miser had given him only a penny.

Just as the rabbi was about to leave, the miser said, "Wait. You have touched me so deeply that I want to give you more money." He disappeared into his house and came back with another penny. The rabbi showered him with more blessings, and the miser soon gave another penny. And so it continued until the rabbi received all the money for the ransom.

During the wedding celebration, the students asked why the rabbi had put up with such behavior. He answered simply that he understood what others did not. Remember the first penny and how dirty it was? That was because for years the miser had held on to it because no one would accept it from him. A penny was all that he had the strength to give, and yet people believed that he was capable of giving more. The rabbi accepted his gifts as the miser was able to offer them, and he blessed his giving regardless of how much was being offered.

I could not get this story out of my mind. I started to question whether to give the sermon I had prepared or whether to tell the story of the penny. On the morning of the holiday, I was still debating about this when I went into the sanctuary to prepare the Torah scroll for the reading of scripture. A young man who worked in the office was there, and I began to tell him of my dilemma. As I took the Torah from the ark, I noticed a penny wedged in the breastplate that adorned the Torah. I screamed, "Oh my God, Jim, it's a sign. I am supposed to give the sermon about the penny." Jim looked at me and politely said, "I'm sure whatever you do, Rabbi, will be fine." I continued my chatter about the pros and cons of the two sermons and went to return the Torah to the ark. Inside the ark was a nickel. I took this to mean that God was telling me, *"I said, give the sermon about the penny."*

So I did.

Why was I compelled—or commanded—to give the sermon about the penny? What did I learn from it about my own life? What could I teach from that story to others about the nature of living and giving? To me, this was a sermon not about money, but about our expectations of giving and receiving. Was I confronting someone with false expectations of what they were capable of giving?

As I asked these questions, my mind drifted to a conflict I was having with a friend. I had trusted him with my friendship and love, and he had let me down. He hadn't even responded to me as I attempted to understand what had happened. A voice suddenly whispered to me, "He's doing the best he can." My anger began to fade. My sense of betrayal stepped back a few paces, and I began to observe his behavior. What if he wasn't mean, angry, or even dishonest? What if he was doing the best he could? I remembered his eyes that used to smile at me in friendship. I saw his stiffness as he now backed away from me. I imagined his fist slowly opening to reveal a dirty penny he had coveted for years. I was asking for unlimited time and affection, and he was handing me what he was capable of giving. Expecting more, I got angry at him and decided he was not a true friend. The more I pushed, the more he retreated. He was doing his best to give me the most. I was the betrayer; I did not accept the gifts that he offered me. This incident taught me that in all the times I had been disappointed by others who fell short of my expectations, these people were actually doing and giving what they could. I had expected more than what they were capable of giving.

The universe abounds with gifts. Receive. Open your heart and receive them. Have no expectations. Stay present as bits of grace fall your way. Be grateful for all you receive, expect little, and accept all that is given with good intention. Penny by penny, moment by moment, the universe provides, and we must learn to accept.

PERSPECTIVE

For Rabbi Charisse Kranes z"l

As you travel a path
Toward a goal,
A goal you deem worthy and essential,
And you suddenly hit a wall,
What you do next depends on your perspective.
The wall is a challenge and you climb.
The wall is failure and you dig a hole to crawl beneath.
The wall is an obstacle, you bang your head.
Or
Upon the wall there is a sign which beckons you to detour.
You turn your head sharply to the left and go another way.

Perspective is the eyesight of your mind.
It is how you choose to look at the world, events, and possibilities.
I have seen lives transformed
When people make the choice
To see things a different way.

THE BEAUTY OF CIRCUMSTANCE

Truth is Beauty and Beauty is Truth—that is all
Ye know on earth, and all ye need to know.
—JOHN KEATS, ODE TO A GRECIAN URN

BEAUTY AND TRUTH DO not lie only in lofty ascents and moments of transcendence. Our life's journey begs us to notice that truth lies in the mundane, for it is the ordinary that we encounter most often. The true challenge is to see the extraordinary in everyday life and to notice God in the mundane.

To do so, Samuel Coleridge asked us to "suspend our disbelief" so that we may enjoy a good metaphor, so that we may see levels of meaning. The literal can be flat like a Formica tabletop. But as you lean on its texture and are supported by its consistency, the table can be a metaphor for that which supports you. Suspend your disbelief. Everything can be packed with meaning— "an outstretched arm" means God will save you. God's messages can be in the metaphor. Not everything is what it seems to be. Slow down and consider the levels of meaning. These slowed frames are God moments.

A real-estate agent I know attended a Sisterhood breakfast class where we were learning about blessings. She told us this story:

"One Sunday I entered a home I was trying to sell. I was alone. I walked into the living room as I had many times before and suddenly froze. I'd been in this home 100 times, but suddenly I noticed the way the sun hit the hardwood floor in a way I never had before and I saw its beauty for the first time. It was as if I saw God in shades of light and wood." Her eyes came back to our class. She was embarrassed. She laughed and turned red. The rest of us were inspired.

One cold March in Chicago, I was wandering in Marshall Fields department store with my friend. We were searching for a place to sit and talk. We had so much to tell each other. She had come all the way from Denver just to talk. We had stories and adventures and new revelations to relate. Instead, we got lost in the fluorescence of retail. Suddenly we came upon a Liz Claiborne fashion show.

"Did you sign up?" asked a lovely lady who was showing people to their seats. "No, but we would like to join you," we said. The lovely lady handed us a gift bag. We giggled at our good fortune. I looked inside the bag and pulled out a perfume sample. The cardboard holder read:

> *Vivid*
> *It's a face lit by*
> *An inner*
> *Brilliance.*
> *A willingness to commit . . .*
> *A readiness to laugh and love.*
> *Vivid*
> *The essence of being.*

I looked at my friend's face. It was vivid with the essence of being. Shifting in my seat, I continued to search the gift bag, and I pulled out a little black notebook. Thrilled with the invitation to write, I wrote this prayer:

God,
Teach me to understand that laughter and love are
The essence of my being and
That Your work is everywhere.
You send messengers to nudge my mind
Into greater awareness.
Thank You, God, for Your many blessings.

Suddenly everything had meaning: perfume, fashion, love, friendship. We left in the middle of the show, having received what we came for: the knowledge that life is good in all its detail and variety.

There is beauty in circumstance. Pause at any given moment. Notice the events and the people around you. Whisper to yourself: *Where is the beauty in this moment, in this set of circumstances?* In the very instant in which we pause, any circumstance can astound.

COINCIDENCE

A man found Joseph wandering in the fields and asked,
"What are you seeking?"
—GENESIS 37:15

My LIFE IS A journey, a searching between points of pause. I seek calm, love, perspective, abundance, faith, and grace. In this journey, there are no chance encounters. Every morning, I say a blessing: "Blessed are You God, Ruler of the Universe, who has brushed the sleep from my eyes." Every morning, I try to see things anew in the crisp morning light. This should always be our prayer: that we open our eyes to see creation as a magnificent tapestry where all things, people, and events are connected, that we increase in our awareness and see that everything that happens guides us closer to what we seek.

In the Bible, Joseph is looking for his brothers to tell them of a dream that he has had. The brothers envy Joseph and are angry at his dreams, which always seem to put him in a superior light. On his way to find the brothers, Joseph gets lost and runs into a stranger who asks if he can help. Joseph asks him if he has seen his brothers, and the stranger directs him to them. Had Joseph not met this man, he may not have found his brothers, an encounter that set into motion a chain of events that eventually led to the great event at Mount Sinai. Who was this man? How did they cross paths? Was their meeting merely a coincidence?

As we reject coincidence, we increase wonder. We see that our lives are guided, and this lessens our feeling that we are a bit lost. There is no coincidence in a world where all things are intertwined. There is no chance in a life that seeks to learn to grow. Poets see all juxtaposition as poetry, all contrast as ironic commentary.

I have a friend who is truly a soulmate. We have loved each other, grown with each other, supported each other for over twenty-three years of life. We are very different. She grew up Italian Catholic in a blue-collar city, and I grew up Jewish in a suburb of Washington. She is single, and I am married with three children. We travel different paths and in different circles, and had we not been roommates our freshman year of college, we would never have met.

I graduated high school a year early and spent the seven months following graduation in Israel on a kibbutz. I received an application and a letter from my parents encouraging me to apply to a university. I applied to one school, the school my boyfriend attended. I applied too late to receive dormitory housing, so I needed to search for a room off campus. I returned from Israel, and my parents and I were at the school the day the list of approved off-campus housing was distributed so that we could find an apartment close to the university. Our zeal landed me a nice room for two across the street from the campus. Carol, on the other hand, had been accepted to the university in plenty of time to receive a room on campus, but a series of mishaps led her to the room we eventually shared. The guidance counselor at her high school said that she would handle the paper work needed to get on-campus housing, but she didn't follow through. Having missed the deadline, Carol was forced to search for off-campus housing. She went to the approved housing that was closest to the university (which was the one that I had rented), but the landlady said it was no longer available. She continued to look the whole day. Tired and disappointed, she called her mother, who told her that the landlady of one of the apartments had called to tell her of a cancellation. Apparently the young woman who was to share the room with me found a better arrangement. Carol immediately went to the building and secured the room. We became roommates for one semester and soulmates for life. Events and people in your life coincide to create the story of your life, but there is no chance in the coinciding.

Be aware, watchful of a stranger on his way: he may have just shown you a path that you might never have taken otherwise. Everything and everyone in our lives are part of our journey. The quest for a spiritual life is in finding the connections in the beautiful tapestry of our life, noticing how the gold thread meets the blue thread to form the perfect picture. Through the perspective of a spiritual journey, there is no chance crossing. Everything has meaning.

The beauty in the sublime and the mundane is found in the perspective that there is no real difference between them.

FOCUS

Rabbi Shimon said,
Three who eat together mindfully,
Attending to talk and taste
And sharing words of Torah and Truth—
It is as if they dined with God,
For God is Reality and Reality is ever present.
All we need do is attend.
—WISDOM OF THE JEWISH SAGES 3:4,
TRANSLATED BY RABBI RAMI SHAPIRO

WE USUALLY THINK OF the thoughts in our head as random, like streams of air we breathe that happen to form words or images in our mind. We believe these thoughts are unconnected, out of our control, often ignored, sometimes maddening. But our thoughts support our beliefs and our assumptions about the world. They reflect and support what we believe is true. We tend to get what we focus on: the cynic finds that people disappoint him; the nurturer sees the world as loving.

I received a notice from the local hospital that a congregant whom I will call Hope was recovering from a stroke. I looked her up in my temple's database and saw that she had a single membership in the synagogue, though we knew she was married. When I called her house, her husband answered in a gruff tone. I said, "This is Rabbi Kedar. How is Hope feeling?"

"Just a second," he replied and put me on hold. A few minutes later, he returned to me, "Who did you say this is?"

"The rabbi from the temple. I wanted to know how Hope is feeling. Is there anything we can do?"

"She's fine. No, we don't need anything."

"May I come and see her?" I asked, sensing his hostility while trying to keep a calm tone of voice. We settled on a mutually convenient time, though I felt that he was not pleased.

On the day I was supposed to see Hope, her husband called the office to give a message to "the lady rabbi" that today was inconvenient. Since I had not spoken to Hope, I persisted. Finally, Hope told her husband she would like to see me, and I scheduled a visit. On the morning of the appointment, I called to confirm the time, and Hope's husband told me to park behind his garage door. I said that I would be over in ten minutes. When I arrived at their apartment, I pulled behind the garage door, but something told me not to park. As I pulled away to look for another space, the garage door opened, and a car pulled out in a hurry. I finally parked my car and entered the house. Sitting in Hope's living room, I found a beautiful woman with a deep sense of spirit and love. This was not what I expected after having only hostile, negative encounters with her husband. She told me this story:

> When I met my husband, he insisted that I convert to Judaism. When I agreed, with the condition that I embark on a serious course of study, he warned me that he would not attend the classes and that I was not to go too far with this "Jewish thing." I found the study to be fascinating and spiritually nurturing and insisted that we celebrate some of the holidays. I would light Hanukkah candles, and he would stand in the doorway, watching from afar. I wanted to attend High Holy Day services, but he refused to join a temple. I started going with my friend whose husband also wouldn't go to ser-

vices. I came to the first service you led at the temple and felt full of love and God. I wrote a letter to the other rabbi telling him of the moving experience I had, and he called me and asked me why I wasn't a member. I didn't tell him that my husband refused to join. Instead, I said that I couldn't afford a membership. He insisted I join with reduced dues, and I did, as a single member. My husband warned me that the rabbi was probably out for my money. Before I had the stroke, I had never seen my husband cry and be so supportive. I know that I will recover fully. Through inner strength and God's help, I make it back more each day.

We continued our talk, and she continued to inspire me. But the source of her husband's hostility still bothered me. I asked her about his family. She told me that his father had died when he was a teenager. Suddenly, I understood his anger. He was angry with God for taking his father. He had held tightly to that anger for years. Yet there was a small crack of light inside the harshness of his soul. He yearned to heal and could not do it himself, so he had married this incredibly spiritual woman to be as near as he could to goodness and beauty and inner peace.

That morning, Hope's husband had left the apartment when he heard I was coming. Our cars had passed in the driveway. He could not be near me, since I represented the "cause" of his father's death. His thoughts about me, my role, and what I was really about supported a belief that he had held on to for many years. This man continues to create the reality that God is the enemy and will never help him or support him. His thoughts about me were not random. With his father's death, he perceived anyone connected with religion to be at fault.

Hope believed I could comfort her. We prayed and cried tears of inspiration.

Her husband believed I was worthy of his suspicion. When I arrived, we passed without a word in separate cars at the entrance to his garage.

We tend to get what we focus on.

The day is judged as bad or good depending on our focus.

The other day, I had this conversation with my teenage daughter:

"How was school today, Talia?"

"Horrible. My math teacher is so annoying."

"But how about the rest of the classes?"

"Oh, they were great."

"You judge the entire day at school on one annoying hour. Maybe we should focus on the other six."

Talia sighed, "Easier said than done."

The next day, we had this exchange:

"How was school today?"

Pause. "OK, I guess."

"Were your classes interesting?"

"Yes."

"Was math annoying?"

"Yes."

"But the day was good overall?"

"I guess so."

Failure and success are often a matter of perception and focus. During the 1998 Winter Olympics, the bronze-medal winner in speed skating was interviewed. He was very upset with his performance. He repeatedly said that he had failed. You saw his agony in achieving third place. He had worked his whole life for the gold medal, and now all those years resulted in perceived failure. The next interview was with the American sixth-place winner. He was ecstatic. He saw his race as a huge success. He had worked all his life to skate his personal best at these games. He was excited and honored that he had done so well in the race. Who failed—and who succeeded?

Focus is a powerful spiritual tool.

What if I collected my thoughts like scattered wildflowers to form a bouquet of beauty? What if I changed the negative in my life just by focusing on the good? I acknowledge the negative thoughts, the thoughts that support fear, sadness, feelings of inadequacy, and then immediately focus on the blessings, the beauty, lessons learned from the challenge. Easier said than done, as my daughter said? I have come to believe that a life of joy is easier than a life of fear and suspicion, or at least more fulfilling.

Do you want to imagine a world of goodness and vitality? Focus on goodness and vitality. Do you want to reach your destination safely? Keep your eye on the road. Do you want to transcend fear? Focus on hope. Do you want God to come to you even in the most ordinary time? Invite God's presence with your words and the kind of company you keep.

Why are we aware of God in our sanctuaries and not in our living rooms? Because it is in our sanctuaries that we direct our thoughts toward God. Invite God into the living room, and you create holy moments and holy space. Focusing is hard. But your mind is powerful. And when it listens to the desire of your soul for beauty and love, your thoughts can transform your reality.

EXPAND YOUR BOUNDARIES

God will expand your boundaries as was promised.
—DEUTERONOMY 19:8

IN THE SYNAGOGUE WHERE I work, there is a couple, Anita and Shel Drobny, who donated a large sum of money to a university to establish a Judaic Studies department. The university was putting together a videotape promoting the new department. The couple said that their love of Judaism and Jewish learning, as well as the example they wanted to set for their children, was the motivation for their generosity. They therefore asked that their rabbis be filmed in the sanctuary as part of the tape.

Under direction of the film crew, we posed with the Torah, taking it out of the ark, opening it, pretending to read from it. At one point, they wanted to film my colleague reading from the Torah by himself. I sat down and watched the TV monitor. As I was observing the art of filmmaking, the retakes and the different angled shots, my mind started to wander to a problem I was having with a friend. I couldn't seem to figure out how to change a very negative pattern we had established. Suddenly, I looked at the monitor and saw that the cameraman had focused on a verse in the Torah: "expand your boundaries." Instantly, I realized that I had been seeing the problem in a very narrow way. I understood that if I

58

expanded my idea of what was possible and what was right, then I could find a solution. I was so overwhelmed with the way in which I had this revelation that I excitedly told everyone present what verse the camera had focused on. No one shared in my enthusiasm; the message was just for me.

Expanding or breaking down barriers is an important spiritual lesson. We often place barriers or boundaries before ourselves that keep us from growing and moving. One prime example of this is the way my parents responded to a desire I had as a child: One morning when I was about eight years old, I wandered into the kitchen. My long brown hair was wild from a night's sleep. My oversized furry pink slippers shuffled across the yellow linoleum floor. Mom was at the sink. I looked up at her and announced, "I want to be a rabbi." There were no female rabbis in those days. But my mother's comment charted the course of my life, "That's nice, dear. Now go get ready for school." For me, her comment was ordinary, not revealing for a moment that my dream was fantastic, extraordinary, or impossible. It was fine. Just as any other dream. Implicit in her pronouncement of "fine" was her permission to dream on. She could have said, "Girls don't do that" or "Are you crazy? What kind of a job is that for a nice Jewish girl?" Decades later, she did voice her fear to me that the lifestyle and demands of the job seemed frightening to her. But when I was eight, she just affirmed it to be as legitimate as any dream I had. In fact, as I grew up, I remember my father saying over and over, "You know Karyn, there's a void out there. The only reason there is a void is because people assume that they can't step into it. But I tell you that you need only to take your place to fill it."

This attitude of my parents was one of my earliest spiritual lessons: the doors that bar us from our dreams are imaginary. If you do not see them, you will walk right through them. Franz Kafka's story "Before the Law" is about a man who spends his entire life trying to gain access to "The Law" and is prevented by a doorkeeper. At the end of the story, Kafka writes that the man

. . . has not very long to live. Before he dies, all his experiences in these long years gather themselves in his head to one point, a question he has not yet asked the doorkeeper. He waves him nearer, since he can no longer raise his stiffened body. . . . "Everyone strives to reach the Law," says the man, "so how does it happen that for all these many years no one but myself has ever begged for admittance?" The doorkeeper recognizes that the man has reached his end and, to let his failing senses catch his words, roars in his ear, "No one else could ever be admitted here, since this gate was made only for you. Now I am going to shut it."

I was taught never to build imaginary doors or gates to keep me out.

We must be aware of building gates that keep us out and maintaining boundaries that keep us in. Saying that life is a journey is more than a cliché. It is a perspective. We must not fear to venture beyond our most basic assumptions of what is true and possible. Go forth into the unknown, with faith and courage and, most of all, with an expanded vision of who you can be.

FORGIVENESS

Forgiveness is the Great Mother of
Inner peace and calm.
The wrongs of the world hold you prisoner
When your heart can not
Release the pain.

To forgive is the ultimate act of self-love.
Forgive out of kindness to yourself
And out of the recognition
That despite all the anger and confusion,
God is everywhere.

GIVE AWAY YOUR ANGER

Rabbi Mikhal gave this command to his sons:
"Pray for your enemies that all may be well with them.
And should you think this is not serving God,
Rest assured that, more than all our prayers,
This love is indeed the service of God."
—MARTIN BUBER

I LOOKED AT MY WATCH impatiently. My lunch companion was late—again. I was on a tight schedule, and in my impatience I found myself pacing between the parking lot, baking in the Florida sun, and the cold air conditioning of the restaurant. Finally, I put on a sweater and settled down inside, ordered a cup of coffee, and watched for my friend. "I am so sorry I'm late," she said as she rushed to my table thirty minutes later. The moment I saw her, I forgave her. I couldn't wait to tell her about a class I had just taught.

We were studying texts on forgiveness, and I had developed an idea that seemed exciting. She listened to me, periodically objecting to a phrase or comment. But mostly she stared at me as if she disagreed in the most fundamental way.

"What's wrong?" I asked her.

"You know," she said slowly, "my mother was murdered."

"Yes," I said. Though I had known this for a while, I had never asked for the details, preferring to wait until she felt comfortable telling me.

"Well, it was my father who killed my mother."

My mind was as blank as my stare. Any thought I had on forgiveness vanished.

"He's sitting in prison, sick with cancer," she said. "He wants to see me. I struggle between the thought of seeing him and never seeing him again. Do I forgive him before he dies? Is it possible to forgive him?"

I began to stutter some cliché. Then I stopped and looked at her eyes. They lacked the emotion and passion I was used to seeing from my friend.

"Can you continue to live with the anger?" I asked. "I'm sure he is less affected by your anger than you are. But what does the anger do to you?"

"When anger overpowers me," she answered, "I feel as if I have relinquished my powers and that I am no longer in control of my life."

"Relinquish your powers," I said, "and you will lose the stuff that makes your life magical. In order to return to a life of wonder, then perhaps you need to find the way to forgiveness."

That afternoon I learned more about forgiveness than during all my years of teaching and study. I began searching for new definitions, new terminology. Old formulations simply no longer applied.

My friend helped me understand that to forgive is not to condone or excuse. There are acts that are inexcusable. There are behaviors that are not to be condoned. But we shouldn't use this truth to keep us angry or fearful. Anger and revenge are destructive. We were born to be creative.

My friend and I continued our conversation over many months. She could not decide whether she should see her father again or not. Finally I said to her, "Forgiveness is not about fantasy. No one expects you to go back to a loving father-daughter relationship."

"What do you mean?" she asked.

"You need not reestablish a relationship. In fact, there are times that you forgive and get out of the way. When you forgive, there is a great internal transformation. You are changed. Your perspective is different. But your father may be just the same. He may have ignored the opportunity for change and be unaffected by your transformation. If that is the case, get out of his way."

To forgive is not an act of kindness toward the person who has wronged you. Forgiveness is an act of kindness toward yourself. It is not about what your offender deserves; it is about what you deserve. We all deserve a life without fear and anger. We have greater things than anger to feel. And to forgive is to rid yourself of anger, fear, and obsession. Imagine the relief of not feeling those things. Just imagine how much energy you would have for creative endeavors if you were not obsessed. Imagine the thoughts you could entertain if you were not thinking, avoiding, plotting angry deeds. It is called "for*give*ness" because you *give* away anger and resentment. To surrender your anger is not to capitulate, or to lose ground, or to give in. Surrender to a softer place, a place of peace, not strife. At the moment of surrender, you realize the beauty of your own path. That it was not only the obvious blessing that helped your life emerge, but also the struggle. When anger is replaced by forgiveness, you are free to let love guide your life.

FORGIVE YOURSELF

You shall love your neighbor as yourself.
—LEVITICUS 19:18

As WE STRIVE TO love others, we often forget to love ourselves. It is as if self-love is forbidden. But actually it is *commanded* in the Bible. The command is not only to love our neighbor, but to love our neighbor *as* we love ourselves. As we deepen the love for ourselves, we deepen the capacity to love others. Love heals. It heals the wounded soul, it heals the relationships we cherish, it heals the world. Self-love strengthens our ability to be loving beings.

We have so many regrets. There were so many times that we could have—or should have—chosen a different path or gone in a different direction. Every time we use the word "should," we accuse ourselves of not doing our best. Every time we say "I could have," we second-guess ourselves, blaming ourselves for not choosing a different path. Guilt and regret are heavy on our souls. Imagine how much energy we would have if we did not let them weigh us down: energy to create, energy to love, energy to move on.

I was recently having coffee with someone who had been a friend for many years. Every time we get together, we begin by recounting the story of our lives, as if we were telling some sacred narrative. At one point, we began to wonder how life would have been different *if we only.* . . . We looked at each other and instantly recognized that we had it all wrong. We were wrong to regret any part of the story. The "good" decisions and the "bad" decisions were all the "right" decisions because they led us down a path that was filled with meaning. There were so many lessons learned from the mistakes, so much growth from the bad experiences that we honestly wouldn't change a moment. "Should have" and "could have" were futile phrases that did not recognize that *all* is for a reason and that we did the best we could at the time. "It's not enough to forgive others," I said. "We must forgive ourselves." For the next several hours, we retold the "sacred narrative," this time recounting the lessons in the turns in the road. "That's what 'repentance' means in Hebrew," I said. "The word for repentance is *teshuvah* and it means to turn toward the right path, the path that leads to an understanding of God."

She smiled. "Then let's *turn* from accusation toward understanding. In the turning, we can head for the goodness of God. Let's take 'should' and 'could' out of our vocabulary."

As we chatted, we became more inspired to understand the choices we had made and began the process toward self-forgiveness. Together, we wrote this prayer:

> *God, thank You for helping me see*
> *That each phase of my life is perfect.*
> *That I have arrived,*
> *That I've always been where I need to be*
> *Living perfect moments . . .*
> *With Your help, I relinquish my need to judge.*
> *Embrace my heart as it beats, even as it bleeds.*
> *Help me grow with love, acceptance, and curiosity.*
> *Thank You for lighting my way*
> *For gently illuminating a path in the darkness . . .*
> *Let it now be and always be*

Yet another exquisite phase.
For the crimes against myself, I am sorry.
For all my slips and slides, I forgive myself.

At every stage in my life, I did what I knew how to do. If I would have known better, I would have done better. But every day I must remember to be kinder to myself and more forgiving of my imperfections, because, at every point along the way, I am blessed. Everything I have done and seen has made me who I am in this moment. It's OK to have been me. I forgive.

TO STRUGGLE AND RELEASE

And Jacob was left alone.
And a man wrestled with him until the break of dawn.
—Genesis 32:25

THE DRAMA OF NIGHTTIME angel encounters are the stuff of ancient texts. Jacob sat on a riverbank at night, alone and afraid of the morning, when he will meet his brother, who had become his enemy and had an army of four hundred men with him. Suddenly a stranger appears—perhaps a man or perhaps an angel—and the two wrestle through the night. Jacob is wounded, and as the sun begins to rise, the angel blesses him with a new name. He is no longer to be called Jacob, but Israel, which means "one who wrestles with God."

We sometimes find ourselves in ambiguous moments, as if, like Jacob, we were between two points—where we've been and where we want to go. It is there, at that in-between point, that we struggle. We wrestle with voices, with emotions, with fear, with our need to forgive, with angels sent by God. But like Jacob, we must struggle, even if we become wounded. We must become like Jacob and stand our ground and embrace our essential self, as we wrestle with God.

Two sisters, both of them in their sixties, made an appointment to see me one day. Their father had just died, and they came to share their grief and sense of guilt. The father had been very controlling and interfered with every aspect of their lives. As they described their home and relationships with each family member, I began to see two different styles of coping. One sister coped by shutting herself off from the struggle. She had left her father's home when she was rather young and seemed to have shut herself off from her pain: "I have to get on with life. Dwelling on our relationship is not useful." Even as I heard her say these words, I saw that she was wrapped up in her anger.

The other sister appeared to be trying to understand her own pain. She had been in therapy for many years and was clearly still wrestling with the relationship she had had with her father as a child and as an adult. She had little confidence, and she'd suffered an ugly divorce and the criticism of her sister, who wished she would stop dwelling on negative experiences and get on with her life. The sister who ran away felt the other was too weak and self-indulgent; the sister who struggled felt the other was not in touch with her emotions.

I saw them both stranded on the riverbank of conflict. One refused to engage in the challenge God had placed before her. The other was locked in a hold she refused to release. Neither was ready to forgive their father—or each other.

Don't be afraid of the struggle. See the struggle as God giving you the chance to triumph over difficulty, to deepen, to grow, to forgive. Engage with the demons and with angels. Then release. Cross over the river and journey on.

ELEVATED THOUGHTS

Elevate your thoughts
To the level of your
Spiritual desires.

Consider every word and image
As reaching toward goodness.
When negative thoughts enter your mind,
Observe them as if they are floating by
Like runaway balloons.

Make your thoughts
Prayerful,
Worthy of your spiritual quest.

BLESSINGS

Blessed is the Supreme God,
From eternity to eternity.
Let all the people say, "Amen."
Hallelujah.
—PSALM 106:48

Blessings make you pause and acknowledge beauty, goodness, and God's presence. When we say a blessing, we stop all movement, all thoughts. We notice our breathing, our spiritual self, and our connection to all that is good and holy. For half a second, if we are doing it right, the world falls into sharp focus, and we are centered and armed with a new perspective.

The sages say that we can make 100 blessings a day:

As we bless the bread we are about to eat, we connect to the Source of all sustenance: "Blessed are You God, Ruler of the Universe, who brings forth bread from the earth."

As we bless the magnificence of a rainbow, we remember the wonder of creation: "Blessed are You God, Ruler of the Universe, who is the source of creation."

After slamming on my brakes to avoid a car that wildly pulled in front of me, I say the blessing for being saved from danger:

"Blessed are You God, Ruler of the Universe, who has saved me for all that is good."

Blessings are flickers of light in a soul that forgets to pause for what is truly important. Like the blessing upon waking. What are the first thoughts that enter your mind as you are somewhere between sleep and awakening? Do you wake to weather and traffic reports on the radio or the elbow of a young child who needs you *now*? Does your mind race to the day's agenda—the driving, the meetings, what clothes to wear? Are you thinking that there just isn't enough time for everything? What if the first thoughts of the day included a morning blessing:

I am truly grateful for You God,
Who has restored within me the breath of my soul.

How would each day be different if you began it with gratitude for being alive?

I discovered the power of the morning blessing after the birth of Ilan. Our third child was born in the middle of the night in May seven years ago in Jerusalem. My husband was on a school trip with 100 teenagers on top of Masada, a mountain where 960 Jews attempted to defend themselves against the attack of the Roman army after the destruction of the Second Temple in the year 70. Every year the school would send their seventh graders to learn about the history and story of Masada while climbing at night to see the sunrise from the top. Somehow, I had known I would deliver this baby without my husband present, and I had arranged for a midwife to be with me at the hospital and help with the delivery.

We were in the delivery room of Hadassah Hospital, and all was going well. Jane, the midwife, and I were in a darkened room, and my labor was hard and fast. It was like riding stormy waves of the ocean. Suddenly I thought of my friend Charisse. Charisse had died of ovarian cancer two years before. She and I had been very close. We had named our second child, Shiri, after her. But it was odd that she should come to my mind in the middle of labor. It was if she were trying to warn me that something was wrong with my new baby. I started to yell to Jane that something was wrong. She tried to assure me, but I knew there was a problem. With the strength of a mother fighting for her child, I pushed until the baby was born. Jane placed him on my chest, and I heard a grunting sound. We exchanged anxious looks, and she rushed him to the doctor, who then rushed him to neonatal intensive care. The baby was born with fluid in his lungs and was put on a respirator.

For the next several weeks, I rushed to the hospital every morning to sit by Ilan's side. Unable to hold him, unable to help him, I put my hand through the opening of the incubator and moved two fingers up and down the bumps of his spine. It was the only place on his body that was not connected or covered by wires and things. As I stroked his back, I rocked back and forth to the rhythm of his breathing and chanted a blessing from the morning prayers over and over again:

> *"I am truly grateful for You God, Who has restored within me the breath of my soul."*

During those weeks, every time fear invaded my sanity, I gently pushed it aside and said, "I am truly grateful for You God, who has restored within me the breath of my soul." I survived the ordeal with faith and love. Ilan is now very healthy. Every time I run my fingers down his spine, I breathe in the blessing of gratitude and restored life.

And every morning I wake, I thank God for life renewed.

PRAYER

A prayer of a lowly soul when faint
Pours forth this plea before God:
O God of Being,
Hear my prayer; let my cry come before You . . .
I lie awake; I am like a lone bird upon a roof.
—PSALM 102:1–2, 8

Prayer puts into words my fears and my hopes. Prayer is a poetic reminder of where I want my soul to live. It reflects the yearnings of my deepest desires. It asks me to turn past my self for help and support. It is a metaphor of the thoughts I might not otherwise express. I pray to engage in conversation and communion with God, to connect with the world of the spirit. Prayer elevates my thinking. By doing so, it raises my life to new levels. I do not pray for favors, gifts, or grants. I pray for courage, strength, understanding, and generosity of spirit. I pray for quiet and peace in my soul.

I was going through a difficult time several years ago. I had prayed for my life to be different than it was. That it would have less strife, more gentleness. I prayed that I would live with greater purpose and focus and less scattering of my energies. Suddenly, I was presented with a series of life-altering decisions and choices that were maddening. It was clear that I was being asked to choose between the old way of living and a new and unknown path. During the day, I could drown my fears with the static of mundane living. But the nights were frightening. To sleep, I needed quiet and relaxation, but the voices would chatter on at a hysterical pace. They were irrational, loud, bold, annoying. *"Relax,"* I tried to shout above the crowd in my head. Finally, I would turn on the TV for a middle-of-the-night free-fall into infomercials and evangelical preaching.

I began to say this night prayer from the liturgy:

Grant, O Eternal God, that I may lie down in peace,
And rise up, O Sovereign, to life renewed.
Spread over us the shelter of Your peace.
Guide us and save us for Your name's sake.
Protect us from hatred and plague;
Keep us far from war and anguish;
Subdue our inclination to do evil.
O God, give us refuge in the shadow of your wings.
O, guard our coming and going
That now and always we have life and peace.
Blessed is God who shelters us with peace.

I realized that my last waking thought reflects the truth of my day and that if I fell asleep thinking holy thoughts, my next day would have a bit more holiness in it. If I asked for peace of mind, I would be more likely to achieve it than if I cursed my restlessness. Make prayer a habit, whether you recite the fixed prayers of your tradition or the spontaneous words of your heart. They are the lullaby of a restless soul. They help you connect with the world of the spirit and elevate your thoughts to matters of holiness.

THINK BEFORE YOU SPEAK

God, open up my lips
That my mouth may declare your glory.
—PSALM 51:17

I LOVE TEACHING AT LATE morning brunches. The women who attend them take a couple of hours to pause for matters of the spirit. For one of these brunches on a Tuesday morning late into Chicago's winter, I had prepared a lesson on the meaning of the above verse in Psalm 51. I sat silently watching the women chatter and get their cups of coffee. My eyes scanned the room looking for direction, for a place to begin. The women here were loosely connected by temple affiliation, and most did not know each other. They were different ages and at different stages of life. I saw women who were curious about what I would say; I saw troubled women who came to find answers; I saw women who came in silence and would leave in silence. Just before beginning to teach, my attention turned to one of the women. Slight with hollow, deep-set eyes, she was one of the silent ones. Her face was tight, angry, sad. I began to teach:

There is a little verse that is traditionally said before the major part of the prayer service: God, open up my lips that my mouth may declare Your glory. What if every time we went to speak, we said that phrase first? If before I answered my spouse, I asked if what I am about to say reflects my spiritual aspirations? If before I went to share a story about another person's life, I asked whether it would reflect the holiness in the world? If before I engaged in idle conversation, I said, "God, when I speak, may it declare Your glory"? If you paused before you spoke, would your conversation be different? Would it force you to elevate your thinking toward glory?

When I was done, a few women shared their comments. The more private ones shared their sighs.

Several months later, we had another brunch. The woman with the deep-set eyes spoke up before I had a chance to begin. "You know that verse you taught us, about thinking before you speak? Well, I tried it, and I never realized how many negative thoughts I had. When my words couldn't reflect God's glory, I kept silent. I was very quiet these last months."

Some in the group laughed, for they thought she was joking. But she was very serious. Having said what she needed to say, she fell silent.

A few months after that morning, I heard that she left an abusive relationship.

May God guide her thoughts and words as she ventures toward living a life worthy of glory.

THE QUEST

One too shy to question can not learn,
Nor can the impatient teach.
—*WISDOM OF THE JEWISH SAGES* 2:6,
TRANSLATED BY RABBI RAMI SHAPIRO

IT WAS EARLY MONDAY morning, and my first appointment of the day walked into my office. In her eyes, I saw pain, wisdom, yearning, exhaustion. I was intrigued. I had seen her for over a year. She would come into services to pray or come to a study session on prayer and listen. We never spoke but always made long, silent eye contact. The last time she came to my class, I approached her and said, "I feel as if you want to say something." "Yes," she said flatly. "I do." She didn't elaborate, so I told her to make an appointment.

She began to tell an elaborate story of a car accident, which left her son on the brink of death. His long fight for survival left the rest of her family in chaos. The accident had happened two years ago. It appeared that everyone in her family was on their way to adjusting, except her. She could not resolve the big questions, and she could not reconcile with the changes that had occurred. Her son would never be the same. And she would never be the same. "Why?" she asked, rather irritated. "Why did this happen to my son?"

There are two types of questions we can ask. One attempts to understand the events that happen or do not happen in our lives. The other tries to explore the foundations on which we build our lives, the basic assumptions that we take as truth. The quality of our question directly relates to the quality of our answer. "Why did this happen to me?" is not a good question. In this woman's life, asking "why" had led her to such answers as there is no God, and life is ugly, and events are cruel and arbitrary. None of these gave her peace or advanced her journey to understanding. She received unsatisfying answers because the question was not good.

Suddenly she asked, "What does God want me to understand from all this?" I smiled. It was a better question, but I did not answer it. She had to find the answer to it herself.

To *question* is to seek new understandings. It is to embark on a *quest* that can be magical and spiritually uplifting. It is to seek meaning and reason in the most casual of events and the most difficult of tragedies. It is to call into question fundamental beliefs and assumptions. When you ask good questions, you grow beyond the boundaries of ordinary life and reach toward peace of mind.

Question everything, from the most basic beliefs to the most frightening problems. When you ask a good question, do not force the answer. Ask it out loud to God, to the universe. Release it to the winds of thought, and then go about your day. Answers will come to you in unexpected ways, perhaps in a dream or when driving your car or in the shower or in conversation with a friend. If someone else tries to answer, make sure it clicks deep within you like a piece of a puzzle easing into place. If it doesn't, reject it. Have patience. Ask again and again. Some answers take time. Others come in a flash.

After this woman in my study asked the question, we continued our conversation. Half an hour later, she sat up. "I know what I am supposed to learn from all this: patience. I must also learn that I do not really have control over my life and those I love. I have to learn to relinquish control." She will ponder the answer she received for a very long time and continue to seek understanding and acceptance. Her questioning will lead her toward greater questions and deeper understanding.

Do not seek definitive answers. That kind of truth leads to complacency or blindness. To answer questions is merely to ponder possibilities. It is to say what occurs to you at this moment. It could be this—or maybe it's that. When the rabbis of the Midrash posed a question, they would formulate an answer. Then they would write the phrase *d'var acher*, which means "or you can look at it this way." And what would follow would be an entirely different answer than the one before.

Questioning is a process that can take a lifetime. There are certain questions I have asked for years. Each time I ask them, the answers take me to a new level of understanding.

Question. Ponder. Question again. Consider. Question again.

This is a worthy life's pursuit.

I do not know why this woman experienced tragedy. I do know that the difficult art of questioning will lead her down paths that she may never have discovered otherwise. I believe she will deepen in understanding. I pray that she will find peace.

BALANCE

Befriend the many aspects of self:
Mind, body, soul, emotions
All form a tapestry of beauty
Handcrafted for you by God.
It is the landscape of your life, your true self.
Deny none their rightful place,
Strive for an equal balance of all the parts.

Collect your emotions.
Unbury your soul.
Honor your body.
Calm your mind.

Balance.
Center.
Journey forth with every part of you
In alignment.

PSYCHOLOGY
VS. SPIRITUALITY

Happy is the one who finds wisdom,
And who attains understanding . . .
(For wisdom) is a tree of life
To those who grasp it
And whoever attains it is happy.
—PROVERBS 3:13, 18

MANY FORCES ARE AT work inside us. We have matters of the mind, matters of the spirit, a whirlwind of emotions. We have forces from our past and our present. We feel fear; we feel hope. As we walk a spiritual path, we must not ignore the world of our psyche. And if we delve into that world, we must not forget the demands of the spirit.

At a meeting of clergy and therapists that I attended, the clergy was concerned about when we should refer a congregant to therapy during a counseling relationship. One well-known psychologist characterized a congregant in need of referral as being stuck in a particular place. "If you see no movement toward health," he said, "but rather a persistent sense of pain or sadness, then perhaps you have done what you can and it is time to refer him to a therapist."

My heart began to race: these were the exact words I used when advising people to terminate therapy. I raised my hand. "Actually," I said, "I have come to the same conclusion but from the opposite point of view. I see people who have been in therapy for ten years. They are quite able to recognize and name the events and people in their lives that caused them pain. 'I am this way,' they say, 'because my mother did that or my father didn't do this. I know why I react. Yet, I am still sad. I feel as if there is an overwhelming sense of darkness in my core that I can't get rid of.' I feel that these people have gone as far as they can in the therapeutic relationship and now they must do their soul work to heal."

Where is the balance between "mind work" and "soul work"? We must attend to both. From the most wonderful childhood to the worst years of nightmare, our minds and souls must come to terms with the world within and without. We must try to make psychological and spiritual sense out of things. We are all in search of sense and peace.

It is dangerous to tend to the soul without doing the necessary psychological work. I know a woman who was raped as a child by her uncle. Her adult life has been a long journey in search of peace. She has read books about spirituality, joined classes that taught spiritual principles, meditated, kept journals, spoken to God. When you first meet her, you are overwhelmed with her sense of peace and spiritual connectedness. But if you engage in a long-term relationship with her, you begin to realize that she is controlling you in the name of God. At first it is subtle, but you sense that you are being manipulated to make choices that are not consistent with who you are. You question yourself. She says she channels a spirit from the metaphysical world. She can tell you what is God's will. And she expects you to comply. Jane has done her spiritual work, but she has not done her psychological work. In its extreme, spirituality void of psychology may lead to cults or even mass suicide. Beware of the spiritual path if it does not invite the mind to gauge its sense of reality.

Yet, I have met countless people who have been immersed in the psychological recesses of their past but do not talk the language of the soul. They describe a deadened sensation in the core of their soul: "I have been in therapy for years. Why do I feel so dark and empty?"

Strive for wholeness. Integrate the stories in your mind with the yearnings of your soul. Recognize the complexities of your being and tend, as best you can, to all corners of your life. Walk a path toward beauty and wholeness with mind and spirit singing in harmony. Do not tire of the work ahead. It is the glory of your life's mission to learn and grow and walk humbly with your God.

LISTENING TO VOICES

There was a great and mighty wind, splitting mountains
and shattering rocks
By the power of the God of Being, but God was not in the wind.
After the wind—an earthquake, but God was not in the earthquake.
After the earthquake—fire. But God was not in the fire.
And after the fire—a still small voice.
—1 KINGS 19:11–12

MOST OF THE TIME, our lives lack the drama of earthquakes and violent winds. Most of the time, we simply go along, as we always have. How is it that we get this overwhelming sense that something is not right even when everything appears to be OK? Maybe we have cut off or shut down parts of our being. Maybe we are not listening to all the voices that are there to guide us.

I was walking with my friend along the railroad tracks in our neighborhood early one morning. She was trying to find a way to explain meditation to her students. "What if I ask a student to sit on the floor and the class forms a circle around her? On my cue, people would start reading from pages I prepared on attitudes toward money, the place of food in their life, difficulties in relationships. Then on my signal, they stop and listen to the quiet. *That* would be the quiet of a meditative state."

Yes, I thought, quiet the chatter. I hear the chatter of many voices. Some are friendly; others are not so nice. Some encourage; others criticize. I hear voices of hope and of despair. I hear voices telling me what to do and what I wish I could do. These voices in my head form one large choir. At times, they inspire. Other times, they make me crazy. I have named three different voices that seem to be present in most of us:

There is the "tenor." They may represent voices from our parents, from good teachers, from bad teachers. They tell you that you'll never be good at math, that you'll always be overweight. They urge you to do what you want but always be the best. They tell you to think of money as a mirror of your self-worth or say sweetly that you can do anything you set your mind to.

You've heard these voices. They are that pain in your neck. They nag: "You *should*, you know." "If only you *could*, but you *can't*." "Well, *why* don't you then?"

Then there is the "baritone." The baritone sings from your mind. This is the voice of reason, of the rational, of the logical. The baritone tells you how to accomplish what you need to do in the world. This is the "how to" voice of life, the hardware store of your being—fix it, seal it, hammer in the point, just do it, climb the ladder of success.

Then there is the "soprano." Some call this voice "intuition," a "sixth sense," a "gut feeling," your "heart's desire." The mystics of Safed called it the *Maggid*, The Teller, for it tells you of the God within you. It speaks to your creativity, your destiny, the purpose of your life. It is the still small voice within. It speaks from the center of your being. This whisper speaks to your goodness, to your Godliness. It beckons you to places where you can clearly see God working in your life. It speaks to those secret urgings that you know to be in alignment with joy. It is to be honored. Go into the stillness. The hush of your soul is God whispering sweet nothings in your ear.

Perhaps you are thinking that you have never heard that voice. When the baritone or tenor sings solo or even a duet for a prolonged period of time, even years or a lifetime, then the monotone is very loud and predominates. All other voices are dulled, silenced, bored from disuse, like a muscle that is weak from lack of exercise.

To hear this intuitive voice, you must first quiet the other voices. Meditation helps. Prayer helps. Writing helps. Talking to people who understand helps. Gently naming the voice when it speaks helps.

I heard a talk given by Sonya Choquette, author of *Your Heart's Desire*. She was attempting to demystify the intuitive voice so that people would not be afraid to listen for it. She suggested that we give that voice a name to help us identify it. When I came home, I decided to try the exercise with my daughter Shiri, who was eight at the time.

"Shiri, do you ever hear inside your heart a voice that is telling you what is right and what is wrong, that somehow is guiding you toward good things?"

"Sure," she said confidently. "You mean Victoria."

I was astounded. "Tell me about Victoria."

"Like if I want to take a piece of candy when I'm in a store and slip it into my pocket, Victoria says, 'No, don't do that.'"

"Yes," I said, "that's it. You listen to Victoria, and she will lead you in the right direction."

The next day, Shiri was getting ready for bed. "Mom, you'll never guess what happened today. We had a fire drill in school, and the fire engines came. I was really scared. Then Victoria told me not to worry, that some boy pulled the alarm. And Mom, she was right!"

"That's great, Shiri. You keep listening to Victoria."

Shiri paused for a second. "Oh, and Mom?"

"What, Shiri?"

"Victoria told me to tell you that she likes your nightgown."

I looked down at my nightgown and saw embroidered in gold thread the words "Victoria's Secret." "Tell Victoria I said thank you," I responded.

Play with your intuitive voice. Listen for the soprano. She may need coaxing to hit the high notes. Have patience.

This choir is the noise in your mind. At times, it is in beautiful harmony: life works, you have energy, there is a stride to your gait. Suddenly, without warning, the tenors are a bit too loud. Your mind fills with self-doubt. You fall back to old patterns that really don't work.

Or maybe the baritone spontaneously insists on a solo. You find yourself functioning at warp speed: car pools, errands, social engagements, days working late, no weekends, unable to relax. There are not enough hours in the day. You become a workaholic, an overachiever.

This morning, a young woman came into my office. She was pretty, smart, and nicely dressed. "I'm not a member of your synagogue, but I suppose we will join soon," she said, as if that was her credential. "But I wanted to speak to a rabbi. You see, I am very pragmatic and rational, but I love Judaism, especially the traditions and the holidays. How can I reconcile my love for Judaism and my agnostic doubts?"

Our conversation went on for over an hour. She was thoughtful and open and honest. She knew that her life looked perfect: husband, child, good job, lovely home. Yet there was something missing. I suggested that if she was bothered by the lack of spirituality she felt, she could begin to discover it by listening for the voice of the spirit from within. I told her that her rational voice was functioning very well, but her creative voice—her intuition, her "God whispers"—were not being heard. When she heard this, she was quiet. Her rational mind wanted to dismiss my words. But she did not give it voice. She had begun the process toward balance between the rational and the spiritual.

You are the conductor of your life. You can bring the choir in your being to new levels of brilliance. Align your past beliefs and assumptions with who you really are. Balance the "doing" and the "being." Let the intuitive voice guide your journey, the rational voice tell you what to do to make it work, and the nagging voice challenge you to struggle, which can help you emerge into beauty.

This is my prayer:

May I be at one
With the various parts of myself.
So that mind and heart work together.
So that the conversations in my head
Form a choir in perfect harmony.
So that what I do is supported by my
Heart's desire
Like a shadow dancing behind a child
At play.
To be connected to the world,
Inspired by the sun and the wind.
To realize that every breath is a gift
And every blizzard has its place.
To be embraced by love for the people in my life.
So there is no fear, no suspicion, no separation
There is only love.

THE INNER TWINS:
LIVING WITH PARADOX

Rebekah conceived
And the children struggled within her
And she said, "If this is so, how can I live?"
—GENESIS 25:21–22

MONDAY, 9:30 A.M.: A man begins to tell me about a difficult divorce. He spares no details. He is a therapist. As I try to offer my thoughts about moving beyond anger, he stops me and says, "I know all that. I tell my clients that all the time." Then he blurts out, "I feel like such a hypocrite. On one hand, I counsel people with similar problems. On the other hand, I cannot resolve my own."

Monday, 10:30 A.M.: A woman comes into my office to tell me that she doesn't believe in God. I don't believe her, for I have seen her trying to come closer to God. I question her, and she begins to explain. Suddenly she exclaims, "How can I send my children to Sunday school and go to prayer services when I'm not even sure of what I believe? When I go to services with them, all I do is cry. I can't wait for it to be over. I feel like such a hypocrite."

Monday, 12:00 noon: A man leans toward me in my study and, in a voice barely audible, asks me, "Am I a hypocrite if I prepare my son for bar mitzvah, but I still don't convert? I never thought it important until now. My wife has never been involved in Judaism. It is up to me to take our child to lessons and services. Do I have the right to tell him to take Judaism seriously when I don't take steps toward becoming a Jew myself?"

After this third appointment, I close the door and smile. Not believing in coincidence, I understand this series of appointments as a message: "I guess I am supposed to learn about hypocrisy today." There are many days when I, too, struggle with the principles I try to teach. I teach one thing, I feel another. Am I a hypocrite?

The people who came into my study that day taught me yet another level of paradox. We are surrounded by paradoxes. People ask: Why am I so sad if my life is so "perfect"? Why do I stay with my spouse when my soulmate beckons me to his side? How can he be mean in his personal life and compassionate in his public life? If I am so good, why am I not succeeding? The answers are as complex as the questions.

We all have paradoxes deep within us—two truths that seem to contradict. They attest to the complexity of our inner lives. Sometimes we bury these inconsistencies. When we do this, we live with an unsettled feeling that people do not know who we really are, as if we are impostors of sorts. Sometimes we judge these paradoxes as hypocrisy. But this I know is true: hypocrisy is a judgment and this judgment, like all judgments, is unkind and does not further our inner peace. If we abandon judgment, we find acceptance of life's complexities.

We seem to have this gnawing desire to lay out our lives like an unshuffled deck of cards where all is clear and in plain view and Queen follows King and the Joker may be wild but it's in its place. Life does not work that way. Life is not neat; the soul is riddled with paradox.

As I am thinking all this, I suddenly remember a year when I discovered a paradox that made me think that I might be losing

my mind. It was the fall before I was to leave for Israel for a sab-
batical. I met a woman named Raven in New Orleans. She had
stringy orange hair and a nose ring. I do not remember her eyes.
Raven told me that the year in Israel would be a difficult year
for me, one dedicated to being and not doing. She said that
during it, I would not be measured by my outward accomplish-
ments, but I would gather inward experiences. There would be
few external demands and distractions and many internal rumblings. I was not to question too much and not overanalyze. I
was just to live and to be. I would deepen, shed a skin, and form
a new one.

Raven was right. That year introduced me to the complicated
world of paradox, to a surrealistic world of opposites. I was pleased
to have time to be with my family, to enjoy simplicity and a
slower pace. But I was also crazed with boredom and uneasiness. I
loved to have the time to think, yet I dreaded hearing the voices
in my head.

The noise and thunder of early morning made me crazy as the
five people in my family were running in different directions: bickering, eating, combing, zippering. By 7:30 A.M., I was exhausted
and tense. Then they left. The door closed, and the noise gave way
to the solitary clicking of the clock. I breathed. I sipped a cup of
coffee. For a split second, I thought to myself that this must be the
best moment of the day. The worst moment of the day and the best
moment of the day were all in the first hour of the day.

Then the silence got to me. The silence was maddening. My
head came alive with screeching voices talking in conflicting
directions. I thought that perhaps I was going mad. So I tried to
drown out the noise with TV and radio. Better other people's trash
than mine. I realized that during all those years of working I had
never had the chance to sort out my own thoughts, uninterrupted
or distracted by the noise of the world. I did not know how to
begin. So I stared, listening to the chatter in the background, trying to deaden the sounds inside.

I called this "boredom." "How are you?" friends asked. "I am bored," I answered. But it was not boredom at all. It was much more complex. I was living a paradox. I had inside me two imaginary twins: a dark-eyed wild girl running through the woods so as not to be discovered and a golden-haired child who was happy to bask in the open fields of contentment. No, I was not bored. The dark-eyed girl was in flight, not wanting to enter the darkness of thought, with its scary creatures lurking in trees and high grass.

Meanwhile, the golden-haired child was calm and peaceful.

How could that be? How could I be both at the same time? Then I learned this truth. Running from our contradictions paralyzes us.

Slowly, I became less afraid of the dark-eyed girl and the woods she frequented, and I remained grateful for the peaceful moments offered by the golden-haired child. Here were contentment and restlessness, avoidance and understanding, running and confronting. Dark-eyed girl and golden-haired child played different games in separate fields, yet both were me.

What a rare opportunity it is to be aware of who you really are without the distractions of what others need you to be. I was present, doing little, covering vast ground, pulling at my hair, and smiling softly.

SUSTAINERS

The people
In your life mirror your world.
If they are hollow, dull, or cruel
So will you see your life.
If they are loving, inspirational, and supportive
You will reflect their beauty.

It is most important
That the company you keep
Reflect the life you wish to live.

Choose your companions wisely,
Seek your teachers well,
Consider carefully the ones you engage
In serious conversation.

Look into the eyes of those who surround you
And you will see a reflection of yourself.

FINDING A SPIRITUAL GUIDE

And the Israelites arrived
At the wilderness of Zin, on the first new moon.
The people stayed at Kadesh (Holiness).
Miriam died there.
The community was without water.
—NUMBERS 20:1–2

IN THE MIDST OF a desert journey leading to freedom, a great prophet and poet named Miriam died in a place called Holiness. They say that wells of water followed Miriam in her travels, allow-ing the Israelites to drink. They say that it was Miriam who brought song and dance to a time of endless sands. They say that it was Miriam who saved her brother's life and taught him love and the need for healing. And then she died and the wells dried up and Moses, blinded by grief forgot, for a time, to believe in goodness.

Miriam was a teacher, a spiritual guide.

To embark on a spiritual journey, you need a spiritual guide. Choose carefully.

A spiritual guide makes "soul talk," the kind of words that pene-trate your heart as true. She fascinates you with topics that lead you to places lovely and strange. She may push you to challenge old beliefs, to redefine what used to be obvious. She does not engage you in therapy. Therapy may be useful at certain junctures of your life. One function of therapy is to help name those events and people that have affected us deeply. But naming is not always enough.

Recently, a woman grabbed my arm after a class and said, "I have been in therapy for years. It has helped me move through difficult issues. Now I know that I react this way because my father did this or my mother didn't do that." She looked into my eyes with pain. Softly, I said, "Now it's time to do soul work. It is time to heal." We talked God, purpose, meaning, love, fear, beauty, soul whisperings, and journeys. Therapy can be a good, important, necessary part of the process, but a spiritual guide ventures beyond the psychological to the poetry of the soul and speaks to the wisdom we already possess, knowing that deep in all of us is the knowledge that we need for our journey.

A spiritual guide is a teacher of the soul. A good teacher draws from what you know in your soul and brings that knowing into words and thought; a good teacher coins a phrase that makes you smile or sigh as you recognize its truth. Yes, you find yourself saying, this makes sense. Good teachers do not claim to be the sole possessor of Truth. They admit to being fellow journeyers. They do not insist that you abandon your family or your life. They do not manipulate. They spin tales that are somehow familiar because they resonate in your core as beauty.

Your quest for inner peace requires a community: friends who know you're not crazy, teachers who urge you on. As the rabbis of centuries past wrote, "Acquire yourself a friend. Find yourself a teacher." If you are open, you will find many guides, many friends, many teachers. Your spiritual guide will lead you to the wells of Miriam, to the miracle of healing.

I search for the Miriam who will lead me to water and to song. She dances in the souls of my friends and my teachers. God, help me find the teachers who will quench the thirst in my soul, who will teach me compassion, who will lead me to Holiness.

RECOGNITION
OF SUSTAINERS

After some time the Wadi dried up, because there was no rain in the land.
And the word of God came to . . . [Elijah]:
"Go at once to Zarephath of Sidon and stay there.
I have designated a widow there to feed you."
So he went at once to Zarephath.
When he came to the entrance of the town
A widow was there gathering wood.
He called to her,
"Please bring me a little water in your pitcher and let me drink."
—1 KINGS 17:7–10

I SAT BACK IN MY tan leather chair and looked around the room. The Sunday morning class included many people whom I didn't know personally. I wondered: What were their stories? Who are they? Why are they here? I scanned the room for people I knew. They smiled at me with warmth and trust. I began to teach the Elijah saga. God told Elijah to go to a distant town where he would find a widow who would give him drink. As he entered the town he recognized her, though they had never met.

How did he know it was her? He asked her for water, and she brought it to him, so his instinct was confirmed by her actions. But there was an initial voice that said to him that *she's* the one, ask her.

Suddenly, one of the new students stopped me abruptly: "How did Elijah know that the widow he saw was the one that God told him to find?" I glossed over the question with some irrelevant answer, but she persisted: "How did he *know?*" I stopped and looked into her eyes. She was an attractive woman in her fifties: bright and articulate and sensitive. She was searching for a deeper answer. Her question was good. How do we recognize the people in our lives as sustainers of our good, nourishers of our soul? I restated the question in that way, and she smiled. It was her turn to sit back: she had been heard.

We all hear that same intuitive voice that Elijah heard. We may walk into a room and scan it before taking our seat among strangers. We look into their eyes, see how they are dressed, the way they hold their head and sense: "No, not next to him. Well, maybe next to her." And then we speak to somebody and just know that he will understand, that it is OK to tell that person a bit more than we might tell someone else.

This is a part of the search for sustainers, those people who will understand, support, and love us. It is a vital search. We can not progress on our journey surrounded by people who do not support us.

I met a woman some time ago whose life had been riddled with abuse. Her father had been verbally abusive to her as a child, always pointing out her faults and telling her that she was not good enough. She married a man who was very similar. He was intelligent and a good provider. He was even fun to be with a good deal of the time. But he had a dark side, which he let loose on her, criticizing her, disapproving, and being angry with her. Her son seemed to take on many of his father's qualities, and her relationship with him was also difficult. She came to me tired, angry, fed up. "I have lived in darkness for so long," she said, "that I just want to live in light and calm. I've had enough." We talked about the importance of sustainers. For her to advance to a place of calm and love, she needed to surround herself with people who supported that vision of herself. Up until now, she had surrounded herself with people who supported her dark side, her pain and inadequacy. "I have changed nearly all of my friends," she said quietly. "I realized that they were mostly negative people. I have few friends now, but they have a more positive outlook." She paused. I let the room fill with her thoughts. "My friends," she said, "now support the good inside of me."

It is so important to rid your life of naysayers: of those people who think that your dreams are impossible, who see what you lack, not what you have, who place limitations on love, growth, and life, whose cynicism supports suspicion and unhappiness.

Invite people into your life who will circle you with love. Their friendship will be like water to your soul. They will see your good even when you don't. When you look into their eyes and into their heart, you see yourself at your best.

"I love you," I once said to a friend.

"Why?" he asked.

"Because I love myself when I am with you."

He brought out the best in me. He allowed space for me to shine and grow.

In the prayers, we say that God sustains the world with grace. The Hebrew word for "sustain," *m'chakel*, has as its root "vessel." The image is beautiful. Our entire world is a beautifully constructed vessel overflowing with God's grace. So, too, should you imagine that your heart is a vessel filled with love and grace. Surround yourself with people who sustain that image as you venture on.

COMMUNITY

Hillel said:
Do not separate yourself from the community.
Do not judge others until you stand in their place.
Do not say that which should not be heard,
For in the end it will be heard.
—MISHNAH AVOT 2:4

THE DESIRE FOR COMMUNITY is not necessarily the search for friendship. It is the search for shared responsibility. The word "responsibility" bids you to respond according to your ability: if you can, respond when I am sick, respond when I give birth, respond when I bury my father. When we have shared moments of celebration and sorrow, we respond by showing up.

In the hours before Hurricane Andrew struck the mainland in southern Florida in the year 1992, the sky was the color of mustard, and the stillness in the air made millions of people hold their breath. A 200-mile-an-hour wind was approaching the coast. My husband and I were renting a townhouse in Boca Raton. Our three small children were with us and I was scared. Around nine o'clock that evening, we walked outside. The neighbors were standing around. We didn't know each other, and nobody said a word.

Never had my need for community been so great, and never had community been so absent. I wanted to reach out: What part of the house was the safest place to be when the storm struck? What were the chances of the eye of the storm hitting where we were? Instead, we were surrounded by isolation and silence.

Community comes from the word "common." The word assumes an awareness that we share in the most basic way: tears, loss, love, illness, joy, fear, birth, death, life. We are not meant to live alone. We are not supposed to ignore or deny what we have in common as human beings. That is the power of community. It is the acknowledgment of the universals of life, the sameness, the common ground. It is the knowledge that I will never be alone when I am sick; that I can share the mixed emotions I will have when my children go away to college; that when I pray for the secret desires of my soul, I will be joined by others doing the same. I live amid strangers, acquaintances, friends, and even a few people whom I don't like. What makes us a community is the sense of shared responsibility: when one is in need, the other simply responds.

I believe that to be fully actualized as an individual, you must belong to a larger community, a community that requires that you break down walls of isolation, a community that will respond to you—and that will ask you to respond in kind.

SURRENDER

Surrender to the mystery of life
And in doing so
Open your heart to Divine wisdom.

Surrender to that simple place of knowing
Where in the softness and calm
God speaks to you.

Surrender to your desire
To believe in goodness and beauty and love
For in all these are Godly waves of truth.

To surrender is not to relinquish responsibility.
Tend to what is yours, release what is God's
Learn to live with ambiguity.

There is a force stronger than your will and ego.
Have faith.
Surrender.

FAITH

Behold,
God is my salvation.
I will trust and not fear.
—HAVDALAH, THE PRAYER FOR THE END OF SABBATH

I HAD A DREAM. MAYBE it was a night vision, for there was no plot, no sequence, no characters. There simply was a picture of a needle and thread sewing two pieces of dark velvet together. When I woke up, I had a thought so clear that I can still hear the echo of a voice in my heart saying, "If you would only learn to sew, you could heal your life." I rarely remember my dreams, so I was excited, even though the meaning completely eluded me. That morning I was scheduled to teach my beloved Sunday class, "Breakfast with the Rabbi," whose name had been aptly changed by my students to "Digressions in Jewish Living." I told them about my dream. They looked at me quizzically. We spent fifteen minutes trying to interpret it, but none of the explanations caused me to sit up straight in recognition.

A year later, I heard this story:

Many years ago in a far-off town, there lived a man whose business was on the brink of ruin. He had one opportunity to save his fortune, and so he traveled to a neighboring town to arrange a business deal. As luck would have it, this man made 500 rubles that day, and it was exactly enough to keep him going. He was on his way home and decided to stop in to see his rabbi. His rabbi greeted him and exclaimed, "How good it is that you come to see me at this time. I must have 500 rubles to give to an unfortunate family in town."

"Rabbi," he said, "you know that I never deny you anything. But please, this time is different. You see, I must have these 500 rubles to save my business. Please understand. I will give it to you as soon as I am able."

But the rabbi would not give in to his pleading, saying, "If you give me your last 500 rubles, I promise you that God will reward you tenfold." After much discussion, the man began to give in. Seeing that he was weakening, the rabbi asked him what he would accept in exchange for the money. The man considered and said, "I hear that there are thirty-six righteous people in the world and because of their righteousness the world is sustained."

"That's right," said the rabbi.

"Well," said the man, "I would like to see one of the thirty-six righteous before I die."

"Granted," said the rabbi, "and may God reward your generosity tenfold."

The man went on his way, and as promised, his business flourished. But the years went on, and he still hadn't met one of the thirty-six righteous. One day, he went to see his rabbi and inquired as to when he would meet one of these great people who sustain the world. His rabbi told him that the time was now.

"Go into the woods. In a clearing, you will see a small house with the light of a candle flickering within. Inside the house lives a tailor. He is one of the righteous that you seek."

Excited, the man rushed to the woods. He wandered in the deep dark for what seemed like a very long time. Finally he came upon a clearing, and he saw a small house with the light of a candle flickering inside. He approached the window and saw a tailor mending clothes. He was about to knock on the door when he thought, "How can I be so bold as to approach the tailor without something to mend." He took his pants and tore them and knocked on the door.

"Come in," said the tailor.

"Will you mend my pants for me?" asked the man.

"Of course," he answered. With that, he took the man's pants and began to sew.

Suddenly, a strange thing happened. As the tailor put the needle in the pants, the man felt a piercing pain. Then the tailor pulled the needle through, and the man felt another piercing pain through his entire body. But when the tailor pulled the thread so that the pants came together, he felt an enormous release. So it continued, a piercing pain followed by a piercing pain that resulted in tremendous relief. Suddenly, the man understood. This righteous tailor, one of the thirty-six who sustain the world, was healing the world through his work. He was doing so first by mending the pants, then by healing this man, and finally by healing a bit of the world.

After hearing this story, I began to understand my dream. I was with a friend in the hospital when the dream became entirely clear.

Joanne's husband was having surgery. He was in his seventies, and the two were extraordinarily devoted to each other. He was very afraid of dying on the table, and she was very afraid of losing him. I was sitting in the waiting room with her, and she looked at me with panic and tears and said, "I just love him so much." I took her hand and said in a whisper, "You know, Joanne, you have done everything that is in your control. You have brought him to the doctor, made sure he came to the hospital, convinced him to have the surgery. You have been by his side feeding him, giving him medication, loving him. At this moment, you must release your control to the skill of the surgeon and the will of God. I once dreamt that there were two pieces of material and that I was to sew them together and that doing so would heal my life. I realize now that one piece of material represented the parts of my life I attempt to understand. It was the life I lead, the moments of clarity as well as the moments of confusion. It was the part of my life with which I struggle to know. The other piece of material represented the part that belongs to God. It is a piece I do not understand and will never understand. My job was to take the two pieces—the life that I struggle to know and the part that I will never know—and sew them together. That is faith, Joanne. Living on the seam that binds together what is in your control with what is not. Living a bit in your world and a bit in God's world. The more we manage to live on the seam, the more we can heal our pain, our fear, our resentment."

We hugged. Her husband survived the surgery.

How do we mend the spirit? Where can we find relief for an aching soul? Healing requires that you open your heart to God's will. It leads to the faith that everything is connected for the highest good of your journey. It begins with letting go of the judgment that we control all events. That is an illusion. We have control only over the bit of our life that is within our grasp. And even then, things are often not what they seem to be.

THE JOURNEY BETWEEN
DESTINATIONS

And Jacob left Beer Sheba and journeyed toward Haran.
He came upon a certain place,
And stopped there for the night,
For the sun had set.
—GENESIS 28:10–11

NEITHER FLEEING NOR GOING, neither here nor there, I am perpetually on my way. I live in the empty space of flight, my life races at an immeasurable rate, never resting in the bull's eye.

This is not a bad place to be—the space between origins and destinations. It is the journey of our lives. Surrender to this journey, and it can show you the beauty of the Divine plan. It was in the empty space of the wilderness that Jacob found God.

Having left his home, his mother, his dying father, his angry brother, Jacob was on his way, he thought, to the land of his grandfather, Abraham, to find a wife and a new home. He left at night, stealing away in darkness. On his way, he became tired. He came upon a certain place and placed a stone under his head. With a stone as a pillow, it seems that his sleep was meant to be fitful.

That night, Jacob dreamt about a ladder that was set on the ground and reached the sky, and the Angels of God were going up and down alongside the ladder. Jacob had this encounter in the vast nowhere of his journey, in that place where we always seem to be: neither at the beginning nor at the end of our journey, but on the way. The angels glided and fluttered alongside the ladder. The ladder's lowest rung snuggled deep in the dirt of the earth, and its height was moist with the dew of heaven. This ladder was meant for Jacob's spiritual ascent. Angels surrounded him, and they danced in his unconscious. They pulled at his memory: remember you come from God, from a promise of great things, from a people who walk with God, who came to a desert town to create a life flowing with milk and honey. Remember that all is possible.

I was teaching my ninth-grade confirmation class. It was early afternoon, and we were all tired. Suddenly I said, "That's it. Get up everyone. Bring paper and pencil. We're going to the play-ground." We went outside, and the students sat on the swings and at the foot of the slide. One climbed the jungle gym. In great detail, I taught them about Jacob's dream. They stared at me. I told them to write down a time when they climbed the ladder. Sitting on the playthings that they used when they were younger, they wrote for about twenty minutes without saying a word. When they were done, I read out loud from their pages. Each told of a moment where they felt a spiritual ascent. They felt inspired by their own lives. I told them to go home and tell their parents about the les-son. These young teens carried the message of spiritual yearning to their homes and asked their parents to tell them when they had climbed the ladder. Some of the parents wrote beautiful, revealing letters. All of them focused on difficult moments of transition in their lives.

This ladder, I learned, does not merely ascend to a higher place. It also symbolizes a transition. It is the spiritual link between where we are—and where we need to go.

I think about this ladder often. It is a powerful image of my soul's yearning to be lifted and carried ever closer to God. Sometimes, in my deepest sigh, I feel this ladder expanding with the air in my lungs. It is the image of my Godly being that urges me to climb, to reach ever higher and further beyond the mundane routine of always. It beckons me to be extraordinary. It calls me to climb toward God with angels at my side. God, I know, is within my reach. I need only grasp the lowest rung.

Venturing into the unknown, even if it is a climb toward goodness, is frightening. As I relinquish my fearful thoughts and surrender to the process and to the journey, my footing becomes more secure.

As I begin to climb, I become aware that God is in that very place, the space between where I have been and where I am going. It is where I live. And I do not live alone.

ALL THAT IS IN
YOUR CONTROL

A gentle response dissipates wrath
A harsh word provokes anger . . .
The eyes of God are everywhere
Observing the bad and good.
A healing tongue is a tree of life.
—PROVERBS 15:1, 3–4

ULTIMATELY, WE ARE NOT in control of our lives. But we act as if we are. We try hard in school to get good grades so we can go to a good university and get the right job and marry the right person so we'll live happily ever after. We think that if only we eat right and exercise enough, we will increase our life span. We make plans, set goals, play the game. Most of the time it goes along OK. Except when it doesn't, and then we know that control is an illusion.

"Of course, you can use my name," Elyssa told me when I told her I wanted to write about her in my book. "Why wouldn't I want you to use my name?" The thought of anonymity puzzled this bright, energetic nine-year-old.

"Well," I tried to explain, "some people want to keep their privacy." As I said this, I knew that the concept of privacy would be strange to her.

"Can I go play video games now?" Elyssa asked abruptly. She was done with our talk and had moved on to more pressing matters. I looked at her brown eyes and big smile and asked her, "Can I say a prayer with you before you go?"

Just two weeks before, I had noticed Elyssa in the crowd of third graders as they sang during services in the temple choir. They were all so beautiful, young, and proud. I noticed Elyssa as she sang every word with great intention as if it all mattered greatly. She had a sense of spirit that drew me to her. I was thrilled when my daughter asked to play with her during the next week.

A week later, I was teaching my Sunday morning adult class when I noticed one of my students was trying to hold back her tears through the lesson. The moment the class was over, she pulled me into the office. Unable—or unwilling—to control her tears any longer, she said, "It's Elyssa."

"Elyssa?" I asked. "What happened?"

"She was playing with a friend. They fell off the couch, and the girl fell on her. All evening she said that she was in pain. Her parents thought that maybe she had broken her leg and took her to the emergency room. When the doctors reviewed the X-ray, they found a tumor that had eaten four-fifths of the bone in her thigh."

I was in shock. Elyssa had just been skating last week. How could this be?

The next day, I called Elyssa's mom, who told me that her daughter would soon be going into surgery and then they would know more. As I was trying to find some words that could give her some comfort, she told me the following story: "When Elyssa was taking her MRI, we were all there watching. In the machine are speakers so we can communicate with her and calm her if need be. Suddenly, we heard her singing from within the MRI. We listened closely, and she was singing Hebrew songs she learned from Sunday school."

I fell silent as tears came to my eyes. I had no words that were more comforting than the song of a child.

So here I was, the day before Elyssa's surgery, trying to offer comfort and a prayer. "What would you say if you prayed?" Elyssa asked.

"I'd ask God to give you courage and guide the hand of your doctor so that he would do a great job. I'd ask that you feel better real soon and that all the bad stuff would stay far away from your life."

Elyssa thought a moment. "Nah," she said. "Can I go play a video game now?" She only wanted the normal, everyday life of a nine-year-old filled with games and fun. She had no time for prayers for the sick. But as I watched her maneuver the stairs on her crutches as she headed toward her games, I felt certain that in the quiet of the night, when nobody was around, she would be saying a prayer.

This is an uncertain world: children get terribly sick, and good people suffer; there are sudden accidents and unpredictable rises to fortune or falls to ruin. We don't know why things happen to us or when they will happen. For Elyssa, falling off the couch while playing with her friend brought her to the hospital and ultimately saved her. All of us ultimately can only control our response to what comes our way. In that way, we make choices about our life at any given moment. Notice the song of a nine-year-old who insisted on play rather than drama. Notice your reactions to life's twists and turns. Choose, as Elyssa, to respond in a way that keeps you steady and hopeful.

MESSAGES FROM GOD

Believe that the universe speaks to you,
And you will be privy to endless chatter.
Believe that God leaves you secret messages to uncover,
And your life becomes an endless treasure hunt.

If you believe that this is nonsense,
Then you will encounter a world that is mute and devoid of guidance.

Messages from God are everywhere.
Listen, watch
Get it on a whisper
God is leading you down gentle paths.

ANGELS

Abraham sat at the entrance to his tent in the heat of the day.
He looked up and saw three angels standing over him.
—GENESIS 18:1–2

I BELIEVE IN THE FLUTTER of angelic life. It's that funny heart-beat. It's the giggle in our souls. It's a candle on a moonless night. It's the mystery behind a faint smile. It makes me sane when I'd rather be crazy. Angels are messages from God. They come to tell us what is important, true, essential, and fundamental. They focus our attention away from daily insanity to simple beauty. They help us center our souls and ground our being so that we can fly in song to God. They can come to us in the form of people we know or people we've just met. They can come in the form of ideas so stark and real that contemplating them leads you right to prayer.

While I was living in Jerusalem, my job became the victim of budget cuts. I went suddenly from a workaholic frenzy to jobless-ness. Joblessness was not just unemployment; it was a suspended state. I had always defined myself through my work, and now I had none. No work meant no self-definition. This is when God sent me angels. I joined the spa at the Jerusalem Hyatt to escape my life. The sauna melted away my defenses. Sometimes I lay alone on

121

a wooden bench dreaming about life's meaning and my purpose under heaven. Or sometimes I sat looking at my friend Aliza, who would tell me about her adventures and discoveries. We were female Huck Finns wandering the swamps of fantasy, wish, and dream. We were friends, though we were very different. I liked her. She liked me.

Amid this heat and sweat, I returned ever so slowly to my dreams and thought I caught a glimpse of an angel or two.

I was most bored in the mornings, when I did not want to clean, write, read, or watch TV. I paced, frowned, and angered easily. I had never had so much time to just *be*. I'd hear my husband say, "Just write." I'd think of a friend saying softly, "Steady girl. Find your center. It's OK. Easy now."

Friends, soul mate types, angels.

My favorite walk was to pick up the kids from school and then go to the store to buy them chocolate milk. I had never taken this walk until that year. I had been so busy with "important" matters of work. While walking, I would squeeze Shiri's hand, and she would squeeze back. This was a silent love ritual we invented that always made us smile. Ilan would run ahead jumping and shooting imaginary guns, feeling safe because his mother was guarding his back. And Talia, my oldest child, would chatter on about fear, love, friendship, and cool leather boots.

Angels. They may come in the form of people if you allow your mind to see. They are messages from God that all is right and truly good.

Or they can be sent to you in the form of ideas personified by such "real" angels as Oriel, Raphael, Gabriel, and Michael. Their names, translated from the Hebrew, describe their essence:

Oriel: "God Is My Light"

I was at Congregation B'nai Torah on the North Shore of Chicago. It was very early on the morning of Rosh Hashanah, a few hours before prayers began. Looking at the point where Lake Michigan kissed the deep blue sky at the horizon's seam, my daughter Talia said, "It's a message from God. God is here right now." I took my shofar in my hand, and with the power of Sinai in my veins, I walked toward the silver morning sun and blew away uncertainty. I said this prayer:

> Good morning, God.
> Thank you for thy abundant blessings
> Give me strength, power, and gently kiss my fears.
> Good, good morning, God.

I remember learning in a college physics class that the light from creation was still shining in the universe. And I thought, yes, I have seen that light. There is a light from without and there is a glow from within, and the angel Oriel flashes between, connecting us to what really matters. It shines when my life is dark. It sparks orange in a nighttime dream as I toss and sweat. It glows a violet blue as I hesitate to walk on an uncharted path. Oriel: God is my light.

> "O God, bless my soul. O God you are truly great . . .
> You wrap Yourself with light as a flowing gown."
> I have seen You on Lake Michigan.

Raphael: "Heal Me, God"

I know that I have been injured. I have been wounded by the stuff of my past, by words and the relationships, the loneliness and the superficial. I have been injured as I descended into danger. Scores of people wounded me with disdain, fear, and indifference. I hurt, as we all do, because it seems at times that life is a failed attempt at grandeur. And that hurts. We have been told to heal the inner child, to heal the wounded spirit, to recover in twelve steps. I join the ranks of the spiritually aware. I call upon Raphael. His name seems strong, romantic, macho. His essence is soft, powerful, nurturing. "Raphael," I say, "heal me. Listen to my prayer, my song, my tears. Heal me, for I bleed."

Gabriel: "God Is My Strength"

No matter how deep my despair, buried in my core is a glimmer of hope named Gabriel. When my joy makes me giddy with life's wonder, there is Gabriel. As I stretch my spirit beyond the familiar, there is Gabriel.

Gabriel: God is my strength as I strive for a life beyond mere survival.

Michael: "Who Is Like God"

As I evoke the image of Michael, I am reminded of the likeness of God within me. It says so in our most ancient text. My soul is God's own image given to me with the breath of creation. In an assembly of second graders, a blonde girl of seven with clear blue eyes asked me very seriously, "How do you really know that there is a God if you can't see Him?" She cuddled against her mother, who wrapped her arm around her daughter's small shoulders. "Does your mommy love you?" I asked. She looked up at her mother and her seriousness vanished into joy.

"Yes," she said.

"How do you know?" I asked.

"'Cuz I know," she said with absolute faith.

"It's the same with God," I said. "You can see God in the same way you see your mother's love, in your heart and in your knowing."

"But what does He sound like?" she insisted.

"God," I said, "sounds like the love in your heart."

Michael: his name means "who is like God"? *We* are.

I am convinced that were it not for angels, my life would be bland and lost. Is that not real death? A life that is bland and lost of all discernible purpose? Is not our only real struggle to fight our tendency to go along in a dull sort of way, without passion, without words of meaning, without poetry, without noticing that flutter in the corner of our eye that tells us we are not alone, that we are loved, that there are angels tugging at us and asking us to come out and play?

THE STARFISH

God said . . .
I set My bow in the clouds,
And it shall serve as a sign.
—GENESIS 9:12–13

Beauty abounds. I have seen it in Lake Michigan when a winter storm brings the mud from the depths of the lake as the waves crash in turmoil. I have seen it in the Judean wilderness where the only sound is from the inch-long wasps as they glide by, lazy from the heat. I have seen beauty in a child's curious conversation flowing in a relentless stream of consciousness. I have seen beauty in the red-stained eyes of a husband as he lingers with the last moments of his dying wife.

There is beauty everywhere the heart permits: in a walk in the woods, in a metaphor discovered, in an encounter with the soul, in the recognition of a secret message revealed. These lead to indescribable moments of beauty where you catch your breath in wonder of the perfection of all things.

The search for beauty leads to paths of peace and contentedness. We can search for beauty in odd places. Every life is a story yearning for beauty. Every event and encounter can be a poetic moment filled with meaning and metaphor, if we only pause to wonder. Sometimes the search for beauty begins with melancholy, that bland feeling that hides the meaning in life.

My friend Linda shared with me a moment that led her to beauty.

It was a stormy, cold day on Sanibel Island in Florida. Linda said that the state of her soul reflected the weather as she set out for a long walk along the beach. She used these walks to regain her spiritual center. She felt sad and alone and disconnected from goodness and peace. Suddenly, she noticed a large, beautiful bird that was diving into the ocean, catching fish, then gliding back in her direction as if beckoning her to follow. She decided to follow it as if it were guiding her to a special place. She followed the bird for what seemed like miles. Suddenly, there was a small break in the clouds, and a ray of light burst onto the beach right in her path. She looked down to where the light hit the beach and saw that a giant starfish had washed ashore. She lifted it up and held it close to her body. At that instant, she was sure that the bird had led her to this place. She felt her sadness disappear. The starfish was a gift from God telling her that she was part of the beauty of creation, that she was loved.

Linda carried the starfish all the way back to the cottage where she was staying. It was heavy, and she struggled with its weight and wetness. When she arrived in town, she took the starfish to a local man who owned a shell store. The man could not believe his eyes. In all the years he had been on Sanibel Island, he had never seen such a thing. This starfish was not native to that area. In fact, it was from the Bahamas. It must have traveled hundreds of miles around the peninsula to reach the shores.

Linda experienced a deep peace upon hearing this. It was as if all details and events had conspired to merge at one perfect moment: the ocean, the currents, the journey of the starfish, the journey of Linda, the cloudy day, the bird leading her down the beach, the one ray of sun shining on the perfect spot at the perfect moment.

Linda dried the starfish, and it is in her library to remind her of God's message to her. She relayed the story to me and our friend Carol years after it occurred. Weeks after telling us this story, Carol received a letter in the mail. She was compiling an anthology about the relationships between granddaughters and grandmothers. One of the people submitting wrote her a letter. The letter was written in longhand: "I am now fifty-eight years old and write in the name of Estelle Peixa, which is a Portuguese idiom. The meaning of this name is Starfish, the creature which regenerates from deep wounds and creates joy."

Carol shared the letter with Linda. "Yes," she said. "When I found the starfish, I felt that, in an instant, my wounds were healed, and there was great joy."

When you open your heart to beauty, you feel less isolated and lonely. You begin to heal. To connect with beauty is to connect with God. It is to recognize a message from God that you are loved.

IS A FLAT TIRE EVER JUST A FLAT TIRE?

In my trouble I called to the Eternal One,
And God answered me.
—JONAH 2:3

"IS THERE MEANING IN everything?" my students asked me during a morning study session.

"Yes," I answered. "I believe there is as much meaning in every event and encounter as we allow ourselves to see."

They were clearly agitated. The journey toward the understanding of life with all its twists and turns and highs and lows can be exhausting. I decided to explore the subject with them: "Do you think that a flat tire is ever just a flat tire? I don't think so."

They shifted in their seats, and I knew that I was losing them.

"I think that sometimes to get through a crisis, we need to turn off our need to understand and simply deal with the situation. But then later, when the crisis is over, we can search for the lessons the event has taught us." I then told them a recent story of a flat tire:

My friend Carol quit her job, packed up her car, and left Denver behind her for a year. She was coming to live with me and write a book about the unconditional love of grandmothers. I was worried about her making the drive to Chicago by herself. I made her promise to check in with me nightly so I could track her progress. One night around 11:00 P.M., I became concerned that I hadn't heard from her that evening.

Suddenly at 11:15, the phone rang. There was Carol—sobbing—on the other end. "Carol, what is the matter? Calm down. Tell me where you are."

"Nebraska," she said. "I was driving the last fifty miles to a motel, and I got a flat tire. I pulled over and it was just so dark I didn't know what to do. I wasn't sure if I should walk to the exit or spend the night in the car."

I was thinking the worst. This was truly a woman's nightmare come true—car trouble in the middle of the night in the middle of nowhere.

"I decided to walk the mile to the next exit," she said. "I just kept saying to myself, 'You are safe. You are safe,' until I reached this convenience store. I walked in and burst into tears. The woman here just hugged me and called a tow truck."

Carol had a tendency for seeing meaning in everything. I was sure that in her hysteria she was reading some weird message in the flat tire.

"Carol, listen to me. When the tow truck arrives and the man takes off your tire and tells you what caused the flat, you believe him. There is no Divine sign here. If it is a nail, then it is a nail. If it is a piece of glass, then that is what it is. This is not a message from God about whether or not you should come to Chicago. It is *just* a flat tire. Do you hear me? Whatever the man says it is, it is."

The man from the local garage changed the tire. It was a nail puncture. The next night, Carol was safely in my home. She was still so traumatized that we just repeated the phrase, "Sometimes a flat tire is just a flat tire." Months later we were talking about the series of synchronicities that led us to be together in Chicago and working on our creative projects. We retold the flat tire story. I said, "I told you at the time that there was no meaning in that event. I told you that because you were in no condition to reflect.

You needed to act. But that whole incident couldn't have been about nothing." She smiled and said, "I was afraid of so many things at that time. How was I going to support myself? Would I really be able to write the book? What would happen to me after the project? Was I irresponsible to quit my job? But mostly I felt alone. Could I really take care of myself? I have no husband, no children. In the middle of all these questions that were so frightening that I couldn't even talk about them, I got this flat tire. While walking on the dark highway with trucks speeding by, I just kept telling myself that I was safe. I think that incident taught me that I was indeed safe and truly capable of taking care of myself during a hard time."

Is a flat tire ever just a flat tire? I don't think so. But sometimes, to get through a crisis, we have to *pretend* that it is. Sometimes we understand events in retrospect, after our fears are calmed. Perspective is gained through time. Meaning is always waiting to be revealed.

LEARNING FROM DEATH

The true worth of a life
Is the story it has left behind.
Tell it well.
Search for meaning and understanding.
Search for truth:
Did he teach you about love?
Did she personify genius or sensitivity?
Did his life warn you of the danger of bitterness and anger?

As I stand and behold the eyes
Of those who mourn, I realize
That the only difference between people in this world
Is not their wealth, fame, or success.
The only difference is
Those who had love in their life
And those who did not.

ON HIS WAY TO MEANING

Life is a journey and
Death a destination to life everlasting.
—RABBI ALVIN FINE

MY LIFE HAS BEEN changed by the lives of people I have never
met. As a rabbi, I have the deep privilege of meeting with families
in their most intimate and sorrowful moments: the immediate
hours after a loved one has died. These moments are very tender.
We sit in my office or in their living room or around the dining
room table, and slowly the life of the dead is created before our
eyes. It is a glorious vision to behold. At first, the details that
come out are facts. Then the words begin to take form, and in the
vision of my heart, I see the person rebirthed, re-created. If I am
patient enough and listen with all my being, what I hear can
inform me of great universal truths about life and our search for
meaning and our longing for love and connection.

I was called on a Sunday to the home of a widow deep in grief.
When I arrived, she greeted me. She was a fragile woman in her
fifties. She had two grown sons, who had arrived from out of town.
We all sat at the dining room table, and one of the sons began to
introduce the family to me. "We are all doctors. My father was a

doctor, as is my mother. My brother and I also went into medicine. We deal with death every day, but this is different."

I smiled and corrected him: "You deal with the dying of the body. Today, you deal with the life of the soul and the death of a loved one."

They smiled, and we both realized that around this table the rational world and the spiritual world encountered one another in the search for meaning and understanding. It was an encounter with which they were not familiar. For about an hour, they talked, I listened, and they cried. The more time that passed, the less comfortable I became. I heard myself saying, "But *who* was he? You have given me a very impressive resume. You have told what he did, who he knew, where he was when each boy was born. But I still don't know who he was."

There was a heavy silence. His wife told me that in college he had minored in religion. The boys looked surprised. They had forgotten that detail, or perhaps they never knew it. I was intrigued. "What question did he want answered?" His wife looked puzzled. "I don't know; we never talked about it." I pressed on. "He was obviously searching to understand something. His life's work involved the study of the brain, and his hobby was the study of religion and philosophy. I see him as driven to understand certain incomprehensible truths."

Apparently, he had never discussed the meaning of life, death, or his search for understanding with his family. For him, these were part of a very private journey that he had traveled alone.

I felt as if I was confronting a puzzle that I needed to solve. What was this man teaching us by the way he lived and the way he died? I suddenly remembered a story they told me that he often repeated:

When he was a small boy, he went with his mother and sister to catch a train. Just as they arrived, the train was pulling away from the station. His mother ran after the train yelling, "Stop the train, stop the train." But the train disappeared down the track. Since that day, this man had two compulsions. The first was to be punctual. In fact, he was so obsessed with being on time that he would arrive terribly early everywhere he went. The second compulsion was trains. As a boy, his father would take him to the train station, and they would sit and watch the trains go by. As an adult, he would travel to Europe and the East, whenever possible, via train. His hobby was building model trains. As a matter of fact, when he died, he was in the process of building a train in his basement.

The day he died, he was coming home from a medical convention with his wife. They were so early for the train for which they had a ticket that they arrived just as an earlier train was starting to prepare to depart. He looked at his wife and said, "Should we run for it?" "Sure," she said. They ran and boarded the train just in time. As the doors began to close, his wife heard someone call for a doctor. She turned and expected to see her husband tending to someone. Instead, he was the one who had collapsed with a massive heart attack. He died instantly.

Here the rational world collides with the spiritual world: there was symmetry to this man's life and death. His obsession with trains carried him through the countries of the world, and it became a metaphor of his desire to travel to places of understanding. He was a neurologist: he studied the brain. He was an amateur philosopher: he studied the mind. This was a man in search of meaning. I learned from him that as I travel through my life, I must strive to understand the secrets of the universe. In silence or in conversation, our mission is to understand.

I mentioned this during his funeral. Afterward, his niece came up to me angry. "The only meaning in my uncle's death," she said, "is that he died of a massive coronary at age sixty-five."

I wonder.

LIVE AS I COULDN'T

Ask the generations past,
Study what their fathers have searched out . . .
Surely they will teach you and tell you.
—Job 8:8, 10

He was a difficult man. Tall. Imposing. Mean when drunk. Very distant. They called him Buzz. Everyone knew that wasn't his real name. Few people knew what his real name was. I knew one of his sons, a kind man named Ron. Ron would tell very funny stories about his family. I always felt that really they were sad. There just wasn't much love, kindness, and attentiveness in his family. I would laugh with my friend while I sent him prayers of love and healing from my heart.

His father took ill—again. They joked how the man had nine lives and was on his tenth. Ron knew that this time it was different. Buzz was deteriorating, and they had to make some hard decisions about his treatment: When was enough enough? When was it time to let him go? I offered to visit Buzz in the hospital, and Ron laughed with sadness in his eyes, "He's not one who cares much for religion. Anyway, he's pretty out of it." I insisted. People change moments before their death, and their soul is often responsive even when their mind is "out of it." Ron gave permission to go, and I went to the hospital looking for Buzz W. The desk found no such name in the computer. We looked and looked, and there was simply no record.

I called Ron. "Did they discharge your Dad?"

"No," he said. Then he began to laugh. "What name did you look up?"

I told him.

"Check Raphael W."

"Raphael? I thought his name was Buzz."

"When he was a child, he was very sick, so they changed his name to Raphael. What's it mean anyway?"

"It means 'God heals,'" I said. If ever there was a person in need of spiritual healing, it was Buzz.

I found this man I had heard so much about sitting in a chair in his room. "Honey, would ya get me my glasses," he said when I entered the room. I brought him his glasses. I introduced myself as his son's rabbi. He rattled on about something unintelligible and seemed agitated that he wasn't getting what he needed. I took his hand. It was dry and red, and his fingers were bent and stiff. He was oddly quiet. I prayed for the healing of the body and soul. He stared at me, then he closed his eyes. I sat there holding his hand, each of us quiet with our own thoughts.

I saw him once more before he died.

The day after his death, I sat with Ron, his mother, and his brother. I had never met his brother. He was quite different from my friend. I felt immediately that he did not laugh away his difficult youth. I tried to get a sense of Buzz from his family. Mostly they told me he was never present. He didn't accomplish much, he wasn't a good provider, and he wasn't an attentive husband or father. I pressed on, looking for something to say at his funeral. I asked the son I had just met for a childhood memory.

"I remember driving to California," he said. "Ron and I were in the backseat fighting. Periodically, Dad would turn around, one hand on the wheel and the other swinging at us, trying to silence our bickering. But mostly, I remember the back of his neck. For hours, I would stare at the back of his neck. It was thick and red with bristles of hair."

I flashed to a similar memory of my own. My family would take yearly road trips to Boston. I would sit behind my father, and he would smile and wink at me in the rearview mirror. I felt like we had a secret game and that I was loved. But Buzz's son saw no smile and no wink. He only saw the hairs on the back of his father's neck. He heard only silence.

When they left my office, I thought about the meaning of Buzz's life: the pain he had felt and caused; the anger he had experienced and inflicted; the love denied, probably for generations.

Raphael: "God heals." His name was his prayer, but it was never pronounced. It was not even known by most people.

On the day of his funeral, I looked into the eyes of his sons. Learn from your father about what is important in life, I told them. If you want a life filled with love, you must love. If you want intimacy, you must reach out to touch those who are at your side. If you want goodness for your children, hold them close to your heart and tell them of their beauty. If you need help, ask for it. Finish the work your father was unable to complete. Ask God to heal your souls and to receive your father in mercy.

Raphael lived a life that was crippled. I feel his hand in mine and hear his soul whisper to me ever so gently: Do it differently.

God, for the sake of our children, heal us.

UNCONDITIONAL LOVE

A woman of valor who can find?
She is clothed in strength and splendor.
—PROVERBS 31:10

RACHEL WAS A SHORT woman who walked with a limp. She had many aches and pains, but I rarely heard her complain. She cooked, cleaned, raised five children, and cared for seventeen grandchildren. Her work began early in the morning and went on into the night.

She was a simple woman. She was also the personification of love and giving.

Rachel was my mother-in-law. Though we came from very different worlds, she lovingly accepted me as Ezra's wife. In the early years of our marriage, I did not understand her. I'd watch her work and work. Her family and I would beg her to take care of herself, but she would just continue to sit at the kitchen table and clean the bag of rice, grain by grain, so that only the purest of food would enter her family's lips.

A week before I gave birth to our third child, she went into the hospital after suffering a stroke. The stroke was considered minor. We tried to encourage her, but she was scared and in pain and did not want to understand. Or did she? How would she manage with one hand and no strength?

I gave birth, and our son had breathing problems and was admitted to the same hospital. Ilan was on the third floor; Rachel was on the fifth floor. She had wanted this baby so much. It would be the first son of her eldest. He would bring honor to this family. I begged her to come and see him in a wheelchair, but she just couldn't find the strength. Ilan was fighting to live; she was preparing to die.

That night, Rachel died of a blood clot in her heart. She was about sixty-five. We were never sure of the exact year of her birth.

With her death, my life changed forever.

She died so suddenly. What did I know of love, of the joy of pure service? At her grave, I prayed that her life would teach me that life is a blessing to live with love and joy. That time wasted in regret and fighting was a sin against my soul.

That was nearly seven years ago. Today, I hear the same story over and over from the adult children who bury their mothers or grandmothers: "She cooked, she cleaned. She quit school when she met my dad. He adored her. There was always plenty of food. Holiday meals at our home were the best. You remember how she made chicken soup? Everybody loved to be in our home. She was always there, making sure we were safe, clean, fed, loved."

Find pockets of unconditional love and live there. Hear the heart of God's intent for our lives. Watch carefully the people you know who simply love and give. Such simplicity is so very complicated for most of us, but they are our teachers, for it is their nourishment, warmth, safety, and love for which we yearn.

CHOOSE LIFE

It is not in the heavens,
That you should say,
"Who among us can go up to the heavens and get it for us? . . ."
Neither is it beyond the sea,
That you should say,
"Who among us can cross to the other side of the sea and get it for us? . . ."
No,
This thing is very close to you,
In your mouth
And in your heart,
To observe it.
See I have set before you this day
Life and death,
Blessing and curse . . .
Choose life—so that you may live.
—Deuteronomy 30:12–15, 19

EPILOGUE: GOD WHISPERS

LIGHT AND GOODNESS ARE not beyond our grasp. We should not defer or postpone joy and blessing. We need only to begin to choose life. A spiritual life, a calm life, a life immersed in love is within our grasp. Reach. All things are connected. The world of the spirit speaks to you in a hundred voices. Listen with the heartbeat of your soul.

Life is an adventure toward beauty. The grandest of journeys begins with a single step. May God bless you on your way.

> *Make the body a throne for the mind,*
> *The mind a throne for the spirit,*
> *The spirit a throne for the soul.*
> *Then the soul too becomes a throne*
> *For the light of the Presence*
> *That rests upon it.*
> *The light spreads forth around you*
> *And you, at the center of that light,*
> *Tremble in your joy.*
> *—Adapted from* Your Word Is Fire, *edited by Arthur Green*
> *and Barry Holtz*

About JEWISH LIGHTS Publishing

People of all faiths and backgrounds yearn for books that attract, engage, educate and spiritually inspire.

Our principal goal is to stimulate thought and help all people learn about who the Jewish People are, where they come from, and what the future can be made to hold. While people of our diverse Jewish heritage are the primary audience, our books speak to people in the Christian world as well and will broaden their understanding of Judaism and the roots of their own faith.

We bring to you authors who are at the forefront of spiritual thought and experience. While each has something different to say, they all say it in a voice that you can hear.

Our books are designed to welcome you and then to engage, stimulate and inspire. We judge our success not only by whether or not our books are beautiful and commercially successful, but by whether or not they make a difference in your life.

We at Jewish Lights take great care to produce beautiful books that present meaningful spiritual content in a form that reflects the art of making high quality books. Therefore, we want to acknowledge those who contributed to the production of this book.

Stuart M. Matlins, Publisher

PRODUCTION
Bridgett Taylor & David Wall

EDITORIAL & PROOFREADING
Jennifer Goneau & Martha McKinney

COVER DESIGN
Drena Fagen, New York, New York

TEXT DESIGN
Susan Ramundo, SR Desktop Services, Ridge, New York

COVER / TEXT PRINTING AND BINDING
Versa Press, East Peoria, Illinois

Spirituality

The Women's Torah Commentary: *New Insights from Women Rabbis on the 54 Weekly Torah Portions* Ed. by *Rabbi Elyse Goldstein*

For the first time, women rabbis provide a commentary on the entire Torah. More than 25 years after the first woman was ordained a rabbi in America, women have an impressive group of spiritual role models that they never had before. Here, in a week-by-week format, these inspiring teachers bring their rich perspectives to bear on the biblical text. A perfect gift for others, or for yourself. 6 x 9, 320 pp (est), HC, ISBN 1-58023-076-8 **$24.95** (Avail. July 2000)

Bringing the Psalms to Life
How to Understand and Use the Book of Psalms by *Rabbi Daniel F. Polish*

Here, the most beloved—and least understood—of the books in the Bible comes alive. This simultaneously insightful and practical guide shows how the Psalms address a myriad of spiritual issues in our lives: feeling abandoned, overcoming illness, dealing with anger, and more. 6 x 9, 208 pp (est), HC, ISBN 1-58023-077-6 **$21.95** (Avail. April 2000)

Stepping Stones to Jewish Spiritual Living: *Walking the Path*
Morning, Noon, and Night by *Rabbi James L. Mirel* & *Karen Bonnell Werth*

Transforms our daily routine into sacred acts of mindfulness. Chapters are arranged according to the cycle of each day. "A wonderful, practical, and inspiring guidebook to gently bring the riches of Jewish practice into our busy, everyday lives. Highly recommended." —*Rabbi David A. Cooper.* 6 x 9, 240 pp, Quality PB, ISBN 1-58023-074-1 **$16.95**; HC, ISBN 1-58023-003-2 **$21.95**

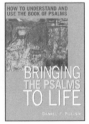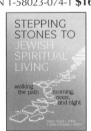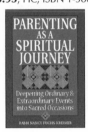

Parenting As a Spiritual Journey:
Deepening Ordinary & Extraordinary Events into Sacred Occasions
by Rabbi Nancy Fuchs-Kreimer 6 x 9, 224 pp, Quality PB, ISBN 1-58023-016-4 **$16.95**

The Year Mom Got Religion: *One Woman's Midlife Journey into Judaism*
by Lee Meyerhoff Hendler 6 x 9, 208 pp, Quality PB, ISBN 1-58023-070-9 **$15.95**;
HC, ISBN 1-58023-000-8 **$19.95**

Moses—The Prince, the Prophet: *His Life, Legend & Message for Our Lives*
by Rabbi Levi Meier, Ph.D. 6 x 9, 224 pp, Quality PB, ISBN 1-58023-069-5 **$16.95**;
HC, ISBN 1-58023-013-X **$23.95**

Ancient Secrets: *Using the Stories of the Bible to Improve Our Everyday Lives*
by Rabbi Levi Meier, Ph.D. 5½ x 8½, 288 pp, Quality PB, ISBN 1-58023-064-4 **$16.95**

Or phone, fax or mail to: JEWISH LIGHTS Publishing
Sunset Farm Offices, Route 4 • P.O. Box 237 • Woodstock, Vermont 05091
Tel: (802) 457-4000 • Fax: (802) 457-4004 • www.jewishlights.com
Credit card orders: (800) 962-4544 (9AM–5PM ET Monday–Friday)
Generous discounts on quantity orders. SATISFACTION GUARANTEED. Prices subject to change.

Spirituality & More

These Are the Words: *A Vocabulary of Jewish Spiritual Life*
by *Arthur Green*

What are the most essential ideas, concepts and terms that an educated person needs to know about Judaism? From *Adonai* (My Lord) to *zekhut* (merit), this enlightening and entertaining journey through Judaism teaches us the 149 core Hebrew words that constitute the basic vocabulary of Jewish spiritual life. 6 x 9, 304 pp, HC, ISBN 1-58023-024-5 **$21.95**

The Enneagram and Kabbalah: *Reading Your Soul*
by *Rabbi Howard A. Addison*

Combines two of the most powerful maps of consciousness known to humanity—The Tree of Life (the *Sefirot*) from the Jewish mystical tradition of *Kabbalah*, and the nine-pointed Enneagram—and shows how, together, they can provide a powerful tool for self-knowledge, critique, and transformation. 6 x 9, 176 pp, Quality PB, ISBN 1-58023-001-6 **$15.95**

Embracing the Covenant
Converts to Judaism Talk About Why & How
Ed. and with Intros. by *Rabbi Allan L. Berkowitz* and *Patti Moskovitz*

Through personal experiences of 20 converts to Judaism, this book illuminates reasons for converting, the quest for a satisfying spirituality, the appeal of the Jewish tradition and how conversion has changed lives—the convert's, and the lives of those close to them. 6 x 9, 192 pp, Quality PB, ISBN 1-879045-50-8 **$15.95**

Shared Dreams: *Martin Luther King, Jr., and the Jewish Community*
by Rabbi Marc Schneier; Intro. by Martin Luther King III
6 x 9, 240 pp, HC, ISBN 1-58023-062-8 **$24.95**

Mystery Midrash: *An Anthology of Jewish Mystery & Detective Fiction*
Ed. by Lawrence W. Raphael; Intro. by Joel Siegel, ABC's *Good Morning America*
6 x 9, 304 pp, Quality PB, ISBN 1-58023-55-5 **$16.95**

The Jewish Gardening Cookbook: *Growing Plants & Cooking for Holidays & Festivals*
by Michael Brown 6 x 9, 224 pp, HC, Illus., ISBN 1-58023-004-0 **$21.95**

Wandering Stars: *An Anthology of Jewish Fantasy & Science Fiction* Ed. by Jack Dann; Intro. by Isaac Asimov 6 x 9, 272 pp, Quality PB, ISBN 1-58023-005-9 **$16.95**

More Wandering Stars
An Anthology of Outstanding Stories of Jewish Fantasy & Science Fiction
Ed. by Jack Dann; Intro. by Isaac Asimov 6 x 9, 192 pp, Quality PB, ISBN 1-58023-063-6 **$16.95**

A Heart of Wisdom: *Making the Jewish Journey from Midlife through the Elder Years*
Ed. by Susan Berrin; Foreword by Harold Kushner
6 x 9, 384 pp, Quality PB, ISBN 1-58023-051-2 **$18.95**; HC, ISBN 1-879045-73-7 **$24.95**

Sacred Intentions: *Daily Inspiration to Strengthen the Spirit, Based on Jewish Wisdom*
by Rabbi Kerry M. Olitzky and Rabbi Lori Forman
4½ x 6½, 448 pp, Quality PB, ISBN 1-58023-061-X **$15.95**

Spirituality—The Kushner Series

Honey from the Rock, Special Anniversary Edition
An Introduction to Jewish Mysticism
by *Lawrence Kushner*

An insightful and absorbing introduction to the ten gates of Jewish mysticism and how it applies to daily life. "The easiest introduction to Jewish mysticism you can read."
6 x 9, 176 pp, Quality PB, ISBN 1-58023-073-3 **$15.95**

Eyes Remade for Wonder
The Way of Jewish Mysticism and Sacred Living
A Lawrence Kushner Reader

Intro. by *Thomas Moore*

Whether you are new to Kushner or a devoted fan, you'll find inspiration here. With samplings from each of Kushner's works, and a generous amount of new material, this book is to be read and reread, each time discovering deeper layers of meaning in our lives.
6 x 9, 240 pp, Quality PB, ISBN 1-58023-042-3 **$16.95**; HC, ISBN 1-58023-014-8 **$23.95**

Invisible Lines of Connection
Sacred Stories of the Ordinary
by *Lawrence Kushner* **AWARD WINNER!**

Through his everyday encounters with family, friends, colleagues and strangers, Kushner takes us deeply into our lives, finding flashes of spiritual insight in the process.
5½ x 8½, 160 pp, Quality PB, ISBN 1-879045-98-2 **$15.95**; HC, ISBN 1-879045-52-4 **$21.95**

   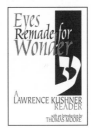 

The Book of Letters
A Mystical Hebrew Alphabet **AWARD WINNER!**
by Lawrence Kushner
Popular HC Edition, 6 x 9, 80 pp, 2-color text, ISBN 1-879045-00-1 **$24.95**; *Deluxe Gift Edition*, 9 x 12, 80 pp, HC, 2-color text, ornamentation, slipcase, ISBN 1-879045-01-X **$79.95**; *Collector's Limited Edition*, 9 x 12, 80 pp, HC, gold-embossed pages, hand-assembled slipcase. With silkscreened print. Limited to 500 signed and numbered copies, ISBN 1-879045-04-4 **$349.00**

The Book of Words
Talking Spiritual Life, Living Spiritual Talk **AWARD WINNER!**
by Lawrence Kushner   6 x 9, 160 pp, 2-color text, Quality PB, ISBN 1-58023-020-2 **$16.95**; HC, ISBN 1-879045-35-4 **$21.95**

God Was in This Place & I, i Did Not Know
Finding Self, Spirituality & Ultimate Meaning
by Lawrence Kushner   6 x 9, 192 pp, Quality PB, ISBN 1-879045-33-8 **$16.95**

The River of Light: *Spirituality, Judaism, Consciousness*
by Lawrence Kushner   6 x 9, 192 pp, Quality PB, ISBN 1-879045-03-6 **$14.95**

Healing/Wellness/Recovery

Jewish Pastoral Care
A Practical Handbook from Traditional and Contemporary Sources
Ed. by *Rabbi Dayle A. Friedman*

This innovative resource builds on the classic foundations of pastoral care, enriching it with uniquely Jewish traditions and wisdom. Gives today's Jewish pastoral counselors practical guidelines based in the Jewish tradition. 6 x 9, 352 pp (est), HC, ISBN 1-58023-078-4 **$34.95** (Avail. Sept. 2000)

Healing of Soul, Healing of Body
Spiritual Leaders Unfold the Strength & Solace in Psalms
Ed. by *Rabbi Simkha Y. Weintraub, CSW*, for The Jewish Healing Center

A source of solace for those who are facing illness, as well as those who care for them. Provides a wellspring of strength with inspiring introductions and commentaries by eminent spiritual leaders reflecting all Jewish movements. 6 x 9, 128 pp, Quality PB, Illus., 2-color text, ISBN 1-879045-31-1 **$14.95**

Self, Struggle & Change: Family Conflict Stories in Genesis and Their Healing Insights for Our Lives
by *Dr. Norman J. Cohen*

How do I find wholeness in my life and in my family's life? Here a modern master of biblical interpretation brings us greater understanding of the ancient text and of ourselves in this intriguing re-telling of conflict between husband and wife, father and son, brothers and sisters. 6 x 9, 224 pp, Quality PB, ISBN 1-879045-64-4 **$16.95**; HC, ISBN 1-879045-19-2 **$21.95**

Twelve Jewish Steps to Recovery: *A Personal Guide to Turning from Alcoholism & Other Addictions . . . Drugs, Food, Gambling, Sex . . .* by Rabbi Kerry M. Olitzky & Stuart A. Copans, M.D. Preface by Abraham J. Twerski, M.D.; Intro. by Rabbi Sheldon Zimmerman; "Getting Help" by JACS Foundation 6 x 9, 144 pp, Quality PB, ISBN 1-879045-09-5 **$13.95**

One Hundred Blessings Every Day: *Daily Twelve Step Recovery Affirmations, Exercises for Personal Growth & Renewal Reflecting Seasons of the Jewish Year* by Rabbi Kerry M. Olitzky, with selected meditations prepared by Rabbi James Stone Goodman, Danny Siegel, and Gordon Tucker. Foreword by Rabbi Neil Gillman, The Jewish Theological Seminary of America; Afterword by Dr. Jay Holder, Director, Exodus Treatment Center 4½ x 6½, 432 pp, Quality PB, ISBN 1-879045-30-3 **$14.95**

Recovery from Codependence: *A Jewish Twelve Steps Guide to Healing Your Soul* by Rabbi Kerry M. Olitzky; Foreword by Marc Galanter, M.D., Director, Division of Alcoholism & Drug Abuse, NYU Medical Center; Afterword by Harriet Rossetto, Director, Gateways Beit T'shuvah 6 x 9, 160 pp, Quality PB, ISBN 1-879045-32-X **$13.95**; HC, ISBN 1-879045-27-3 **$21.95**

Renewed Each Day: *Daily Twelve Step Recovery Meditations Based on the Bible* by Rabbi Kerry M. Olitzky & Aaron Z. *Vol. I: Genesis & Exodus*; Intro. by Rabbi Michael A. Signer; Afterword by JACS Foundation. *Vol. II: Leviticus, Numbers and Deuteronomy*; Introduction by Sharon M. Strassfeld; Afterword by Rabbi Harold M. Schulweis. *Vol. I:* 6 x 9, 224 pp, Quality PB, ISBN 1-879045-12-5 **$14.95**; *Vol. II:* 6 x 9, 280 pp, Quality PB, ISBN 1-879045-13-3 **$14.95**

Theology/Philosophy

Torah of the Earth: *Exploring 4,000 Years of Ecology in Jewish Thought*
Ed. by *Rabbi Arthur Waskow*

Major new resource offering us an invaluable key to understanding the intersection of ecology and Judaism. Leading scholars provide us with a guided tour of ecological thought from four major Jewish viewpoints. Vol. 1: *Biblical Israel & Rabbinic Judaism*, 6 x 9, 272 pp, Quality PB Original, ISBN 1-58023-086-5 **$19.95** ; Vol. 2: *Zionism & Eco-Judaism*, 6 x 9, 272 pp, Quality PB Original, ISBN 1-58023-087-3 **$19.95** (Avail. May 2000)

Broken Tablets: *Restoring the Ten Commandments and Ourselves*
Ed. by *Rabbi Rachel S. Mikva*; Intro. by *Rabbi Lawrence Kushner*; Afterword by *Rabbi Arnold Jacob Wolf* **AWARD WINNER!**

Twelve outstanding spiritual leaders each share profound and personal thoughts about these biblical commands and why they have such a special hold on us.
6 x 9, 208 pp, HC, ISBN 1-58023-066-0 **$21.95**

Evolving Halakhah: *A Progressive Approach to Traditional Jewish Law*
by *Rabbi Dr. Moshe Zemer*

Innovative and provocative, this book affirms the system of traditional Jewish law, *halakhah*, as flexible enough to accommodate the changing realities of each generation. It shows that the traditional framework for understanding the Torah's commandments can be the living heart of Jewish life for all Jews. 6 x 9, 480 pp, HC, ISBN 1-58023-002-4 **$40.00**

God & the Big Bang
Discovering Harmony Between Science & Spirituality **AWARD WINNER!**
by Daniel C. Matt
6 x 9, 216 pp, Quality PB, ISBN 1-879045-89-3 **$16.95**; HC, ISBN 1-879045-48-6 **$21.95**

Israel—A Spiritual Travel Guide **AWARD WINNER!**
A Companion for the Modern Jewish Pilgrim
by Rabbi Lawrence A. Hoffman 4¾ x 10, 256 pp, Quality PB, ISBN 1-879045-56-7 **$18.95**

Godwrestling—Round 2: *Ancient Wisdom, Future Paths* **AWARD WINNER!**
by Rabbi Arthur Waskow
6 x 9, 352 pp, Quality PB, ISBN 1-879045-72-9 **$18.95**; HC, ISBN 1-879045-45-1 **$23.95**

Ecology & the Jewish Spirit: *Where Nature & the Sacred Meet* Ed. and with Intros.
by Ellen Bernstein 6 x 9, 288 pp, Quality PB, ISBN 1-58023-082-2 **$16.95**;
HC, ISBN 1-879045-88-5 **$23.95**

Israel: *An Echo of Eternity* by Abraham Joshua Heschel; New Intro. by
Dr. Susannah Heschel 5½ x 8, 272 pp, Quality PB, ISBN 1-879045-70-2 **$18.95**

The Earth Is the Lord's: *The Inner World of the Jew in Eastern Europe*
by Abraham Joshua Heschel 5½ x 8, 112 pp, Quality PB, ISBN 1-879045-42-7 **$13.95**

A Passion for Truth: *Despair and Hope in Hasidism* by Abraham Joshua Heschel
5½ x 8, 352 pp, Quality PB, ISBN 1-879045-41-9 $ **$18.95**

Theology/Philosophy

A Heart of Many Rooms
Celebrating the Many Voices within Judaism
by *Dr. David Hartman* AWARD WINNER!

Named a *Publishers Weekly* "Best Book of the Year." Addresses the spiritual and theological questions that face all Jews and all people today. From the perspective of traditional Judaism, Hartman shows that commitment to both Jewish tradition and to pluralism can create understanding between people of different religious convictions.
6 x 9, 352 pp., HC, ISBN 1-58023-048-2 **$24.95**

A Living Covenant: *The Innovative Spirit in Traditional Judaism*
by *Dr. David Hartman* AWARD WINNER!

Winner, National Jewish Book Award. Hartman reveals a Judaism grounded in covenant—a relational framework—informed by the metaphor of marital love rather than that of parent-child dependency. 6 x 9, 368 pp, Quality PB, ISBN 1-58023-011-3 **$18.95**

The Death of Death: *Resurrection and Immortality in Jewish Thought*
by *Dr. Neil Gillman* AWARD WINNER!

Does death end life, or is it the passage from one stage of life to another? This National Jewish Book Award Finalist explores the original and compelling argument that Judaism, a religion often thought to pay little attention to the afterlife, not only offers us rich ideas on the subject—but delivers a deathblow to death itself. 6 x 9, 336 pp, Quality PB, ISBN 1-879045-87-7 **$18.95**; HC, ISBN 1-879045-61-3 **$23.95**

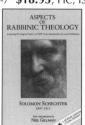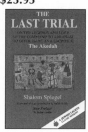

Aspects of Rabbinic Theology by Solomon Schechter; New Intro. by Dr. Neil Gillman
6 x 9, 448 pp, Quality PB, ISBN 1-879045-24-9 **$19.95**

The Last Trial: *On the Legends and Lore of the Command to Abraham to Offer Isaac as a Sacrifice* by Shalom Spiegel; New Intro. by Judah Goldin
6 x 9, 208 pp, Quality PB, ISBN 1-879045-29-X **$17.95**

Judaism and Modern Man: *An Interpretation of Jewish Religion* by Will Herberg; New Intro. by Dr. Neil Gillman 6 x 9, 336 pp, Quality PB, ISBN 1-879045-87-7 **$18.95**

Seeking the Path to Life AWARD WINNER!
Theological Meditations on God and the Nature of People, Love, Life and Death
by Rabbi Ira F. Stone
6 x 9, 160 pp, Quality PB, ISBN 1-879045-47-8 **$14.95**; HC, ISBN 1-879045-17-6 **$19.95**

The Spirit of Renewal: *Finding Faith after the Holocaust* AWARD WINNER!
by Rabbi Edward Feld
6 x 9, 224 pp, Quality PB, ISBN 1-879045-40-0 **$16.95**

Tormented Master: *The Life and Spiritual Quest of Rabbi Nahman of Bratslav*
by Dr. Arthur Green
6 x 9, 416 pp, Quality PB, ISBN 1-879045-11-7 **$18.95**

Your Word Is Fire: *The Hasidic Masters on Contemplative Prayer*
Ed. and Trans. with a New Introduction by Dr. Arthur Green and Dr. Barry W. Holtz
6 x 9, 160 pp, Quality PB, ISBN 1-879045-25-7 **$14.95**

Life Cycle

Jewish Paths toward Healing and Wholeness
A Personal Guide to Dealing With Suffering
by *Rabbi Kerry M. Olitzky*

"Why me?" Why do we suffer? How can we heal? Grounded in the spiritual traditions of Judaism, this book provides healing rituals, psalms and prayers that help readers initiate a dialogue with God, to guide them along the complicated path of healing and wholeness.
6 x 9, 192 pp (est), Quality PB, ISBN 1-58023-068-7 **$15.95**   (Avail. July 2000)

Mourning & Mitzvah: *A Guided Journal for Walking the Mourner's Path through Grief to Healing*
by *Anne Brener, L.C.S.W.*; Foreword by *Rabbi Jack Riemer*; Intro. by *Rabbi William Cutter*

For those who mourn a death, for those who would help them, for those who face a loss of any kind, Brener teaches us the power and strength available to us in the fully experienced mourning process. 7½ x 9, 288 pp, Quality PB, ISBN 1-879045-23-0 **$19.95**

Tears of Sorrow, Seeds of Hope
A Jewish Spiritual Companion for Infertility and Pregnancy Loss
by *Rabbi Nina Beth Cardin*

A spiritual companion that enables us to mourn infertility, a lost pregnancy, or a stillbirth within the prayers, rituals, and meditations of Judaism. By drawing on the texts of tradition, it creates readings and rites of mourning, and through them provides a wellspring of compassion, solace—and hope. 6 x 9, 192 pp, HC, ISBN 1-58023-017-2 **$19.95**

Lifecycles
V. 1: *Jewish Women on Life Passages & Personal Milestones* AWARD WINNER!
Ed. and with Intros. by Rabbi Debra Orenstein
V. 2: *Jewish Women on Biblical Themes in Contemporary Life* AWARD WINNER!
Ed. and with Intros. by Rabbi Debra Orenstein and Rabbi Jane Rachel Litman
V. 1: 6 x 9, 480 pp, Quality PB, ISBN 1-58023-018-0 **$19.95**; HC, ISBN 1-879045-14-1 **$24.95**
V. 2: 6 x 9, 464 pp, Quality PB, ISBN 1-58023-019-9 **$19.95**; HC, ISBN 1-879045-15-X **$24.95**

Grief in Our Seasons: *A Mourner's Kaddish Companion*
by Rabbi Kerry M. Olitzky 4½ x 6½, 448 pp, Quality PB, ISBN 1-879045-55-9 **$15.95**

A Time to Mourn, A Time to Comfort: *A Guide to Jewish Bereavement and Comfort*
by Dr. Ron Wolfson 7 x 9, 192 pp, Quality PB, ISBN 1-879045-33-8 **$16.95**

When a Grandparent Dies
A Kid's Own Remembering Workbook for Dealing with Shiva and the Year Beyond
by Nechama Liss-Levinson, Ph.D.
8 x 10, 48 pp, HC, Illus., 2-color text, ISBN 1-879045-44-3 **$15.95**

So That Your Values Live On: *Ethical Wills & How to Prepare Them*
Ed. by Rabbi Jack Riemer & Professor Nathaniel Stampfer
6 x 9, 272 pp, Quality PB, ISBN 1-879045-34-6 **$17.95**

Life Cycle & Holidays

How to Be a Perfect Stranger, In 2 Volumes
A Guide to Etiquette in Other People's Religious Ceremonies
Ed. by *Stuart M. Matlins* & *Arthur J. Magida* **AWARD WINNER!**

What will happen? What do I do? What do I wear? What do I say? What should I avoid doing, wearing, saying? What are their basic beliefs? Should I bring a gift? In question-and-answer format, *How to Be a Perfect Stranger* explains the rituals and celebrations of America's major religions/denominations, helping an interested guest to feel comfortable, participate to the fullest extent possible, and avoid violating anyone's religious principles. It is not a guide to theology, nor is it presented from the perspective of any particular faith.
Vol. 1: *America's Largest Faiths*, 6 x 9, 432 pp, HC, ISBN 1-879045-39-7 **$24.95**;
Vol. 2: *Other Faiths in America*, 6 x 9, 416 pp, HC, ISBN 1-879045-63-X **$24.95**

Putting God on the Guest List, 2nd Ed.
How to Reclaim the Spiritual Meaning of Your Child's Bar or Bat Mitzvah
by *Rabbi Jeffrey K. Salkin* **AWARD WINNER!**

The expanded, updated, revised edition of today's most influential book (over 60,000 copies in print) about finding core spiritual values in American Jewry's most misunderstood ceremony.
6 x 9, 224 pp, Quality PB, ISBN 1-879045-59-1 **$16.95**; HC, ISBN 1-879045-58-3 **$24.95**

For Kids—Putting God on Your Guest List
How to Claim the Spiritual Meaning of Your Bar or Bat Mitzvah
by Rabbi Jeffrey K. Salkin 6 x 9, 144 pp, Quality PB, ISBN 1-58023-015-6 **$14.95**

Bar/Bat Mitzvah Basics
A Practical Family Guide to Coming of Age Together
Ed. by Cantor Helen Leneman 6 x 9, 240 pp, Quality PB, ISBN 1-879045-54-0 **$16.95**;
HC, ISBN 1-879045-51-6 **$24.95**

The New Jewish Baby Book **AWARD WINNER!**
Names, Ceremonies, Customs—A Guide for Today's Families
by Anita Diamant 6 x 9, 336 pp, Quality PB, ISBN 1-879045-28-1 **$16.95**

Hanukkah: The Art of Jewish Living
by Dr. Ron Wolfson 7 x 9, 192 pp, Quality PB Original, Illus., ISBN 1-879045-97-4 **$16.95**

The Shabbat Seder: The Art of Jewish Living
by Dr. Ron Wolfson 7 x 9, 272 pp, Quality PB, Illus., ISBN 1-879045-90-7 **$16.95**
Also available are these helpful companions to *The Shabbat Seder*: Booklet of the Blessings and Songs, ISBN 1-879045-91-5 **$5.00**; Audiocassette of the Blessings, DN03 **$6.00**; Teacher's Guide, ISBN 1-879045-92-3 **$4.95**

The Passover Seder: The Art of Jewish Living
by Dr. Ron Wolfson 7 x 9, 336 pp, Quality PB, Illus., ISBN 1-879045-93-1 **$16.95**
Also available are these helpful companions to *The Passover Seder*: Booklet of the Blessings and Songs, ISBN 1-879045-94-X **$5.00**; Audiocassette of the Blessings, DN04 **$6.00**; Teacher's Guide, ISBN 1-879045-95-8 **$4.95**

Children's Spirituality

A Prayer for the Earth
The Story of Naamah, Noah's Wife
by *Sandy Eisenberg Sasso*
Full color illus. by *Bethanne Andersen*

For ages
4 & up

NONDENOMINATIONAL, NONSECTARIAN

This new story, based on an ancient text, opens readers' religious imaginations to new ideas about the well-known story of the Flood. When God tells Noah to bring the animals of the world onto the ark, God also calls on Naamah, Noah's wife, to save each plant on Earth.

"A lovely tale. . . . Children of all ages should be drawn to this parable for our times."
—*Tomie dePaola*, artist/author of books for children

9 x 12, 32 pp, HC, Full-color illus., ISBN 1-879045-60-5 **$16.95**

The 11th Commandment: Wisdom from Our Children
by The Children of America

For all ages

MULTICULTURAL, NONDENOMINATIONAL, NONSECTARIAN

"If there were an Eleventh Commandment, what would it be?" Children of many religious denominations across America answer this question—in their own drawings and words. "A rare book of spiritual celebration for all people, of all ages, for all time."—*Bookviews*
8 x 10, 48 pp. HC, Full-color illus., ISBN 1-879045-46-X **$16.95**

Sharing Blessings: Children's Stories for Exploring the Spirit of the Jewish Holidays
by *Rahel Musleah* and *Rabbi Michael Klayman*
Full-color illus. by *Mary O'Keefe Young*

For ages
6 & up

What is the spiritual message of each of the Jewish holidays? How do we teach it to our children? Many books tell children about the historical significance and customs of the holidays. Now, through engaging, creative stories about one family's preparation, *Sharing Blessings* explores ways to get into the *spirit* of 13 different holidays. "Lighthearted, and yet thorough—allows all Jewish parents (even those with very little Jewish education) to introduce the spirit of our cherished holiday traditions." —*Shari Lewis*, creator and star of PBS' *Lamb Chop's Play-Along*
7 x 10, 64 pp, HC, Full-color illus., ISBN 1-879045-71-0 **$18.95**

The Book of Miracles
A Young Person's Guide to Jewish Spiritual Awareness
by *Lawrence Kushner*

For ages
9 & up

From the miracle at the Red Sea to the miracle of waking up this morning, this intriguing book introduces kids to a way of everyday spiritual thinking to last a lifetime. Kushner, whose award-winning books have brought spirituality to life for countless adults, now shows young people how to use Judaism as a foundation on which to build their lives. "A well-written, easy to understand, very lovely guide to Jewish spirituality. I recommend it to all teens as a good read." —*Kimberly Kirberger*, co-author, *Chicken Soup for the Teenage Soul* 6 x 9, 96 pp, HC, 2-color illus., ISBN 1-879045-78-8 **$16.95**

Children's Spirituality

In Our Image
God's First Creatures
by *Nancy Sohn Swartz*
Full-color illus. by *Melanie Hall*

For ages
4 & up

NONDENOMINATIONAL, NONSECTARIAN

A playful new twist on the Creation story—from the perspective of the animals. Celebrates the interconnectedness of nature and the harmony of all living things. "The vibrantly colored illustrations nearly leap off the page in this delightful interpretation." —*School Library Journal*

"A message all children should hear, presented in words and pictures that children will find irresistible." —*Rabbi Harold Kushner*, author of *When Bad Things Happen to Good People*

9 x 12, 32 pp, HC, Full color illus., ISBN 1-879045-99-0 **$16.95**

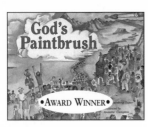

God's Paintbrush

For ages
4 & up

by *Sandy Eisenberg Sasso*; Full color illus. by *Annette Compton*
MULTICULTURAL, NONDENOMINATIONAL, NONSECTARIAN

Invites children of all faiths and backgrounds to encounter God openly in their own lives. Wonderfully interactive; provides questions adult and child can explore together at the end of each episode. "An excellent way to honor the imaginative breadth and depth of the spiritual life of the young." —*Dr. Robert Coles*, Harvard University
11 x 8½, 32 pp, HC, Full color illus., ISBN 1-879045-22-2 **$16.95**

Also available: A Teacher's Guide: A Guide for Jewish & Christian Educators and Parents 8½ x 11, 32 pp, PB, ISBN 1-879045-57-5 **$6.95**

God's Paintbrush Celebration Kit 8½ x 11, HC, Includes 5 sessions/40 full color Activity Sheets and Teacher Folder with complete instructions, ISBN 1-58023-050-4 **$21.95**

In God's Name

For ages
4 & up

by *Sandy Eisenberg Sasso*; Full-color illus. by *Phoebe Stone*
MULTICULTURAL, NONDENOMINATIONAL, NONSECTARIAN

Like an ancient myth in its poetic text and vibrant illustrations, this award-winning modern fable about the search for God's name celebrates the diversity and, at the same time, the unity of all the people of the world. "What a lovely, healing book!" —*Madeleine L'Engle*
9 x 12, 32 pp, HC, Full color illus., ISBN 1-879045-26-5 **$16.95**

What Is God's Name? (A Board Book)

For ages
0–4

An abridged board book version of the award-winning *In God's Name*.
5 x 5, 24 pp, Board, Full color illus., ISBN 1-893361-10-1 **$7.95**

Children's Spirituality

God Said Amen

by *Sandy Eisenberg Sasso*
Full-color illus. by *Avi Katz*

For ages 4 & up

MULTICULTURAL, NONDENOMINATIONAL, NONSECTARIAN

A warm and inspiring tale of two kingdoms: Midnight Kingdom is overflowing with water but has no oil to light its lamps; Desert Kingdom is blessed with oil but has no water to grow its gardens. The kingdoms' rulers ask God for help but are too stubborn to ask each other. It takes a minstrel, a pair of royal riding-birds and their young keepers, and a simple act of kindness to show that they need only reach out to each other to find the answers to their prayers.

9 x 12, 32 pp, HC, Full color illus., ISBN 1-58023-080-6 **$16.95**

For Heaven's Sake

by *Sandy Eisenberg Sasso*; Full-color illus. by *Kathryn Kunz Finney*

For ages 4 & up

MULTICULTURAL, NONDENOMINATIONAL, NONSECTARIAN

Everyone talked about heaven: "Thank heavens." "Heaven forbid." "For heaven's sake, Isaiah." But no one would say what heaven was or how to find it. So Isaiah decides to find out, by seeking answers from many different people. "This book is a reminder of how well Sandy Sasso knows the minds of children. But it may surprise—and delight—readers to find how well she knows us grown-ups too." —*Maria Harris*, National Consultant in Religious Education, and author of *Teaching and Religious Imagination* 9 x 12, 32 pp, HC, Full color illus., ISBN 1-58023-054-7 **$16.95**

But God Remembered: Stories of Women from Creation to the Promised Land

by *Sandy Eisenberg Sasso*; Full-color illus. by *Bethanne Andersen*

For ages 8 & up

NONDENOMINATIONAL, NONSECTARIAN

A fascinating collection of four different stories of women only briefly mentioned in biblical tradition and religious texts. Award-winning author Sasso vibrantly brings to life courageous and strong women from ancient tradition; all teach important values through their actions and faith. "Exquisite. . . . A book of beauty, strength and spirituality." —*Association of Bible Teachers* 9 x 12, 32 pp, HC, Full color illus., ISBN 1-879045-43-5 **$16.95**

God in Between

by *Sandy Eisenberg Sasso*; Full color illus. by *Sally Sweetland*

For ages 4 & up

MULTICULTURAL, NONDENOMINATIONAL, NONSECTARIAN

If you wanted to find God, where would you look? A magical, mythical tale that teaches that God can be found where we are: within all of us and the relationships between us. "This happy and wondrous book takes our children on a sweet and holy journey into God's presence." —*Rabbi Wayne Dosick, Ph.D.*, author of *Golden Rules* and *Soul Judaism*

9 x 12, 32 pp, HC, Full color illus., ISBN 1-879045-86-9 **$16.95**

The Way Into... Series

A major 14-volume series to be completed over the next several years, *The Way Into...* provides an accessible and usable "guided tour" of the Jewish faith, its people, its history and beliefs—in total, an introduction to Judaism for adults that will permit them to understand and interact with sacred texts.

Each volume is written by a major modern scholar and teacher, and is organized around an important concept of Judaism.

The Way Into... will enable all readers to achieve a real sense of Jewish cultural literacy through guided study. Forthcoming volumes include:

The Way Into Torah

by *Dr. Norman J. Cohen*

What is "Torah"? What are the different approaches to studying Torah? What are the different levels of understanding Torah? For whom is the study intended? Explores the origins and development of Torah, why it should be studied and how to do it. Addresses these and many other issues in this easy-to-use, easy-to-understand introduction to the ancient subject.

6 x 9, 160 pp. (est), HC, ISBN 1-58023-028-8 **$21.95** (Avail. June 2000)

The Way Into Jewish Prayer

by *Dr. Lawrence A. Hoffman*

Explores the reasons for and the ways of Jewish prayer. Opens the door to 3,000 years of the Jewish way to God by making available all you need to feel at home in Jewish worship. Provides basic definitions of the terms you need to know as well as thoughtful analysis of the depth that lies beneath Jewish prayer.

6 x 9, 160 pp (est), HC, ISBN 1-58023-027-X **$21.95** (Avail. July 2000)

The Way Into Encountering God in Judaism

by *Dr. Neil Gillman*

Explains how Jews have encountered God throughout history—and today—by exploring the many metaphors for God in Jewish tradition. Explores the Jewish tradition's passionate but also conflicting ways of relating to God as Creator, relational partner, and a force in history and nature.

6 x 9, 176 pp (est), HC, ISBN 1-58023-025-3 **$21.95** (Avail. July 2000)

The Way Into Jewish Mystical Tradition

by *Rabbi Lawrence Kushner*

Explains the principles of Jewish mystical thinking, their religious and spiritual significance, and how they relate to our lives. A book that allows us to experience and understand the Jewish mystical approach to our place in the world.

6 x 9, 176 pp (est), HC, ISBN 1-58023-029-6 **$21.95** (Avail. July 2000)

Spirituality

My People's Prayer Book: *Traditional Prayers, Modern Commentaries*
Ed. by *Dr. Lawrence A. Hoffman*

This momentous, critically-acclaimed series is truly a people's prayer book, one that provides a diverse and exciting commentary to the traditional liturgy. It will help modern men and women find new wisdom and guidance in Jewish prayer, and bring liturgy into their lives. Each book includes Hebrew text, modern translation, and commentaries *from all perspectives* of the Jewish world. Vol. 1—*The Sh'ma and Its Blessings,* 7 x 10, 168 pp, HC, ISBN 1-879045-79-6 **$23.95**
Vol. 2—*The Amidah,* 7 x 10, 240 pp, HC ISBN 1-879045-80-X **$21.95**
Vol. 3—*P'sukei D'zimrah* (Morning Psalms), 7 x 10, 240 pp, HC, ISBN 1-879045-81-8 **$21.95**
Vol. 4—*Seder K'riyat Hatorah* (Shabbat Torah Service), 7 x 10, 240 pp, ISBN 1-879045-82-6 **$23.95**
(Avail. June 2000)

Voices from Genesis: *Guiding Us through the Stages of Life*
by *Dr. Norman J. Cohen*

In a brilliant blending of modern *midrash* (finding contemporary meaning from biblical texts) and the life stages of Erik Erikson's developmental psychology, the characters of Genesis come alive to give us insights for our own journeys. 6 x 9, 192 pp, HC, ISBN 1-879045-75-3 **$21.95**

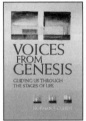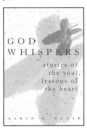

God Whispers: *Stories of the Soul, Lessons of the Heart*
by Rabbi Karyn D. Kedar 6 x 9, 176 pp, HC, ISBN 1-58023-023-7 **$19.95**

Being God's Partner
How to Find the Hidden Link Between Spirituality and Your Work AWARD WINNER!
by Rabbi Jeffrey K. Salkin; Intro. by Norman Lear
6 x 9, 192 pp, Quality PB, ISBN 1-879045-65-6 **$16.95**; HC, 1-879045-37-0 **$19.95**

ReVisions: *Seeing Torah through a Feminist Lens* AWARD WINNER!
by Rabbi Elyse Goldstein 5½ x 8½, 208 pp, HC, ISBN 1-58023-047-4 **$19.95**

Soul Judaism: *Dancing with God into a New Era*
by Rabbi Wayne Dosick 5½ x 8½, 304 pp, Quality PB, ISBN 1-58023-053-9 **$16.95**

Finding Joy: *A Practical Spiritual Guide to Happiness* AWARD WINNER!
by Rabbi Dannel I. Schwartz with Mark Hass
6 x 9, 192 pp, Quality PB, ISBN 1-58023-009-1 **$14.95**; HC, ISBN 1-879045-53-2 **$19.95**

The Empty Chair: *Finding Hope and Joy—*
Timeless Wisdom from a Hasidic Master, Rebbe Nachman of Breslov AWARD WINNER!
Adapted by Moshe Mykoff and the Breslov Research Institute
4 x 6, 128 pp, 2-color text, Deluxe PB, ISBN 1-879045-67-2 **$9.95**

The Gentle Weapon: *Prayers for Everyday and Not-So-Everyday Moments*
Adapted from the Wisdom of Rebbe Nachman of Breslov by Moshe Mykoff and
S. C. Mizrahi, with the Breslov Research Institute
4 x 6, 144 pp, 2-color text, Deluxe PB, ISBN 1-58023-022-9 **$9.95**

"Who Is a Jew?" *Conversations, Not Conclusions* by Merle Hyman
6 x 9, 272 pp, Quality PB, ISBN 1-58023-052-0 **$16.95**; HC, ISBN 1-879045-76-1 **$23.95**

Jewish Meditation

Discovering Jewish Meditation
Instruction & Guidance for Learning an Ancient Spiritual Practice
by *Nan Fink Gefen*

Gives readers of any level of understanding the tools to learn the practice of Jewish meditation on your own, starting you on the path to a deep spiritual and personal connection to God and to greater insight about your life. 6 x 9, 208 pp, Quality PB, ISBN 1-58023-067-9 **$16.95**

Meditation from the Heart of Judaism: *Today's Teachers Share Their Practices, Techniques, and Faith* Ed. by *Avram Davis*

A "how-to" guide for both beginning and experienced meditators, drawing on the wisdom of 22 masters of meditation who explain why and how they meditate. A detailed compendium of the experts' "best practices" offers advice and starting points. 6 x 9, 256 pp, Quality PB, ISBN 1-58023-049-0 **$16.95**; HC, ISBN 1-879045-77-X **$21.95**

The Way of Flame
A Guide to the Forgotten Mystical Tradition of Jewish Meditation
by *Avram Davis* 4½ x 8, 176 pp, Quality PB, ISBN 1-58023-060-1 **$15.95**

   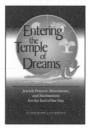 

Entering the Temple of Dreams: *Jewish Prayers, Movements, and Meditations for the End of the Day* by *Tamar Frankiel* and *Judy Greenfeld*

Nighttime spirituality is much more than bedtime prayers! Here, you'll uncover deeper meaning to familiar nighttime prayers—and learn to combine the prayers with movements and meditations to enhance your physical and psychological wellbeing. 7 x 10, 184 pp (est), Illus., Quality PB, ISBN 1-58023-079-2 **$16.95** (Avail. April 2000)

Minding the Temple of the Soul: *Balancing Body, Mind, and Spirit through Traditional Jewish Prayer, Movement, and Meditation*
by *Tamar Frankiel* and *Judy Greenfeld*

This new spiritual approach to physical health introduces readers to a spiritual tradition that affirms the body and enables them to reconceive their bodies in a more positive light. Focuses on traditional Jewish prayers, with exercises, movements, and meditations. 7 x 10, 184 pp, Quality PB, Illus., ISBN 1-879045-64-8 **$16.95**; Audiotape of the Blessings, Movements and Meditations (60-min. cassette) **$16.95** Videotape of the Movements and Meditations (46-min. VHS) **$20.00**

Or phone, fax or mail to: **JEWISH LIGHTS** Publishing
Sunset Farm Offices, Route 4 • P.O. Box 237 • Woodstock, Vermont 05091
Tel (802) 457-4000   Fax (802) 457-4004   www.jewishlights.com
Credit card orders **(800) 962-4544** (9AM–5PM ET Monday–Friday)
Generous discounts on quantity orders. SATISFACTION GUARANTEED. Prices subject to change.